THIS BOOK IS DEDICATED TO

DAVID CLEGG
(BIG CLEGGY)
1978–1997

HIS LOVE OF HADRIAN'S WALL COUNTRY COULD NEVER BE SURPASSED.

THE SPIRIT OF
HADRIAN'S WALL

THE SPIRIT OF
HADRIAN'S WALL

PHOTOGRAPHY BY ROGER CLEGG
WORDS BY MARK RICHARDS

First edition 2008
ISBN-13: 978 1 85284 558 2

Text and maps © Mark Richards 2008
Photographs © Roger Clegg 2008

A catalogue record for this book is available
from the British Library.

Designed by Caroline Draper
Printed and bound by
KHL Printing Co Pte Ltd, Singapore

ACKNOWLEDGEMENTS
Thanks are owed to Mark Richards for his enthusiasm for Roger's photography,
his introduction to Cicerone and invaluable assistance in the production of this
book and to Paul Beniams, prolific Hadrian's Wall guide, with whom Mark has
had many fascinating conversations about the Wall over the years.

ROGER CLEGG
A professional photographer living in Hexham, Northumberland, Roger has
devoted much of the last six years to photographing Hadrian's Wall and the
surrounding countryside. As he explains in 'A Note on the Photography', his
challenge was first to identify all the aspects of the Wall, material and abstract, to
be captured, and then to create a pictorial essay of the Wall, by taking pictures
throughout the seasons, throughout the day, and in all weather and lighting
conditions. His work is founded on his empathy with, and passion for, the Wall
itself and its setting. Just being in the right place at the right time to witness some
of Nature's best and most awe-inspiring displays has been a privilege.
www.hadrianswallcountry.com

MARK RICHARDS
A fascination with writing (and illustrating) walking guidebooks and exploring
wild and historic landscapes has brought Mark to a particular appreciation of
English frontiers. His first frontier guide was to Offa's Dyke, the Anglo-Welsh
border, and then, in 1993, he pioneered a coast-to-coast route – The Wall Walk
– in a guide published by Cicerone. This was a forerunner of the official
National Trail – The Hadrian's Wall Path – to which Mark, naturally, also wrote
the Cicerone guidebook. He is also the creator of the 'From A to B to SEE'
leaflet – a visual interpretation of the journey of the Hadrian's Wall Bus for
inquisitive passengers.
www.markrichards.info

FRONT COVER:
*An iconic view across Castle Nick to Crag Lough
and Hotbank Crags as the morning sun generates an
ethereal mist which veils the low ground and the water*

HALF TITLE:
*A dramatic sunset on Midsummer's Night silhouettes
two fairy walkers under the tree at Sycamore Gap*

FRONTISPIECE:
*Looking along Hadrian's Wall from Kennel Crags to
Sewingshields Crags, the bright summer landscape
contrasting with the darkening clouds above*

FACING TITLE PAGE:
*In the late evening in midsummer, the low, warm light
of the setting sun strikes the top of the Wall at
Walltown Crags*

BACK COVER:
*At Cawfields Crags on a bitterly cold February
afternoon, heavy cloud and patches of sunlight
are chased across the landscape by a fierce
north-westerly wind*

Published by Cicerone, 2 Police Square, Milnthorpe, Cumbria LA7 7PY Tel. 01539 562 069 www.cicerone.co.uk

CONTENTS

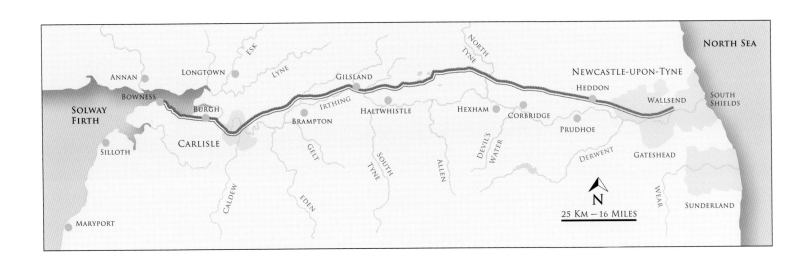

The autumn mists of a cold mid-October evening developing under a variegated sunset over Cuddy's Crags

A NOTE ON THE
PHOTOGRAPHY

Why photograph Hadrian's Wall? Steeped in history and legend, this famous monument runs through the most varied, beautiful, and often dramatic countryside, from lowland pastures to the wild upland crags of the Whin Sill fault, and also passes through the urban cityscapes of Newcastle-upon-Tyne and Carlisle. It presents an interesting and challenging subject for any landscape photographer.

For me personally, it also has a local resonance. By the time this book comes out I will have lived in Hexham, close to the course of Hadrian's Wall, for more than 20 years. And, finally, it is extremely accessible. The whole of the dramatic central section is less than 30 minutes' drive from my home, so I have been able to return again and again to the same spots to capture the Wall in all possible conditions.

A leading photographer when asked 'How do you get those amazing pictures?' responded with 'F8 and be there'. (F8 is a good general aperture setting for many pictures.) In other words, the subject and the photographer are more important than the technology. The technical aspects of photography can be learned from the excellent range of magazines and books, numerous photographic societies and readily available courses. I want to talk here about the 'be there' aspect of my landscape photography.

Once basic techniques have been mastered, success in landscape photography is more about the photographer and less about photography. Before embarking on taking the pictures included in this book I had been interested in photography as a hobby for 30 years. It was a relaxation from a succession of frenetic jobs requiring long hours, much driving and many hotels. I knew a vast amount about equipment and the theory of picture taking. I could tell anyone how to take a masterpiece. The one problem was I rarely took a good picture myself! There was no purpose or discipline to my photography or empathy with my subject. But in 2001, during a prolonged period involving family illness, tragedy and redundancy, I decided to review life and concentrate on photography. The result is the kind of landscapes that you see in this book.

The change from being an uninspiring amateur photographer occurred almost overnight. For the first time I really had to think about the pictures I was taking. They had to have commercial appeal but, more importantly, they had to satisfy my new-found high expectations in terms of creativity and style. (Had I not achieved these personal objectives I would not have continued!)

Each time I took a photograph, I now needed to discipline my considerable technical knowledge to produce a good picture, one that satisfied both prospective clients and myself.

WHEN I WAS FIRST ASKED to supply pictures of Hadrian's Wall I thought 'No problem, I have quite a few already'. Wrong! My stock from my amateur days had pictures taken leaning on Hadrian's Wall and photographing over it, leaning on the Wall and photographing away from it, with the Wall just out of view over the top of the crag or just around the corner, and so on. The Wall itself rarely featured in my pictures of it!

So I defined the images that I wanted to capture and set about creating pictures to satisfy that definition. I created a list of words to describe the Wall – history, myth, legend, wilderness, bleakness, turbulence, beauty, drama, solidity, context, purpose, timelessness, diversity and difference. These are the elements that I have looked for throughout, while answering the deceptively uncomplicated question 'What must this photograph show?' Combined, with my knowledge of the Wall and its moods, I now knew what I wanted before I left home! As is clear from some of the captions in this book, this is not to say that opportunism and good luck have not played its part. But were it not for setting and pursuing these initial objectives with commitment I would probably not have been in the right place at the right time for those 'lucky' moments.

My objective has always been to produce a collection of pictures of Hadrian's Wall that, taken together, capture its character. My hope is that there is a consistency of style that makes them easy to appreciate in this way. Each new picture is not intended as a standalone image but a piece of the jigsaw, fitting in with, and adding to, the whole. I do not take pictures for any great moral, ethical, spiritual or deeply psychological reason; I simply revel in the process of acquiring the picture and derive enormous satisfaction from the results. My inspiration comes from the inherent beauty and drama of my subject.

TWO ESSENTIAL INGREDIENTS of a good landscape photograph are a dramatic or interesting sky and an interesting and informative foreground. The sky is a vital component of any landscape photograph and can seldom be ignored. Whenever possible my rule is – no good sky, no photograph. Equally, whenever possible, a strong foreground is desirable. The foreground tells you about the location and gives a sense of scale; the background shows you where it is.

Once I had embedded this whole new approach to my photography, I suddenly found that I was getting the type of pictures that I had envied from others – those misty mornings, dramatic skies and pictures of interest and impact. I had often blamed others' successes on their good fortune – happening to be in a place where you got that sort of thing. Of course, the reality was that they had made the commitment to hard work, early mornings and uncomfortable weather!

Patience, perseverance and resilience are essential aspects of the landscape photographer's character. You must have the ability to wait for long periods, be disappointed and then come back again and again until you are as close as possible to, or even exceed, your original expectation. A photographer must also be able not merely to look at a landscape but to see into it – to see colour, tone, contrast, perspective, shape and spatial relationships, and then to interpret all these as a two-dimensional design.

I want to create for others the experience of being where the photograph was taken at a particular moment in time – and to distill the combined effect of using all our senses into a mere two-dimensional representation. I want people to ask 'Where's that?'

I have also tried to develop a style to differentiate my photography, as much as possible, from other Hadrian's Wall photographers. This usually requires numerous early mornings and late evenings to catch the best of the day's light, and to be out in weather that keeps many at home. The weather forecast has become an indispensible part of my life. A lot of hard work is consigned to the bin if I feel I am falling short of my own expectations. I have spent incalculable hours along the central part of the Wall waiting for the anticipated conditions to materialise. Frequently they do but just as often they don't and on many days the camera remains securely in its bag.

I know most of Hadrian's Wall very well. I know where the sun sets and rises throughout the year; I know where the mist forms. I know where to go to illustrate the various features of the Wall in its environment and how and when they can best be exploited. Because Hadrian's Wall is confined to a relatively small area I obviously revisit places many times – and the fascination for these much visited locations never declines. They are never the same twice, changing with time of day, weather and season. It is often possible to get a different and original picture.

OVER TIME photography has ceased to be my sole reason for visiting Hadrian's Wall. I have my favourite places – some wild and exposed, some sheltered, all with dramatic views. These are places I will go, frequently when the weather is wild and few others venture on to the more exposed parts of the Wall. Here I may brew a mug of tea or two and just sit. I may reflect on the past, plan the future or just relax and enjoy the elements. Sitting high on Winshields Crags I sometimes reflect on The Beatles song 'Fool on the Hill'. If the drivers far below speeding to work in their warm cars, desperate to make appointments or panicking to get the kids to and from school could ever see me sitting high above in the wind and rain, they would think I was mentally challenged. Look at the pictures in this book and make up your own mind.

On the car radio I once heard a sound recordist relating his experiences capturing the natural sounds of remote and uninhabited parts of the world. This requires long periods of quiet and solitude just listening and looking. In time he said that he began to believe in the spirit of wild places, such as the spirit of the forest. I fully understand this sentiment. Particularly in the wilder places everything in nature seems interrelated – it assumes the behaviour of a single entity. The flora, the fauna, the geology, the weather all exist for each other and because of each other. Change one and the balance is upset. There is a presence that orchestrates and holds it all together. In the countless hours spent along Hadrian's Wall from well before sunrise to well after sunset, or in the more tempestuous weather, I wonder whether I have had the privilege of being in the presence of the spirit of Hadrian's Wall.

Roger Clegg

A breathtaking January sunrise over the Headquarters Building at Housesteads Fort with Grindon Lough as a frosty backdrop.

The breaking cloud and thinning mist reveal the course of the Wall as it meanders over Housesteads, Kennel and the distant Sewingshields Crags

Prudhoe Castle reflected in the pond to the south of the castle. The winter dawn sky throws the buildings of the inner bailey into relief.

INTRODUCTION
THE ROMAN FOOTPRINT

The march of time has left many impressive imprints of man's passing in this land of far horizons. None are more compelling than the Roman footprint and, in particular, the great Wall of Emperor Hadrian. Still surviving today to varying degrees across the country, after almost two millennia of border strife, the Wall gives us a unique link with antiquity. It helps us cast a long backward glance to those literate, cultured people, many identifiable through their inscriptions and writing tablets, living their lives in our familiar landscape. From coast to coast we can imagine the drama of that distant time when the power in the land was formidably foreign and the Celtic tribes were reluctant hosts to the first expression of a greater European union, the Commonwealth of Rome. This book sets out to reveal the magical beauty of this well-known and well-loved remnant frontier, and the tapestry of landscapes through which it runs, through the timeless visual drama of the elements.

WG Hoskins in his seminal work *The Making of the English Landscape* drew attention to a basic truth – that the landscape we see today, the human landscape, is far older than we imagine. Hoskins' survey exposed the inter-generational palimpsest, written and overwritten over the generations, picking out the particular and the peculiar. His book was a melancholy lament to an 'immemorial landscape' as he put it, the inevitable by-product of his appreciation of, and emotional connection with, the people whose lives he revealed. For all of us – the field archaeologist, the academic historian and the likes of you and me – in experiencing historic places of the calibre of Hadrian's Wall we are making outrageously long ancestral connections. The Mediterranean-wide cultural mix of people who made up the Wall's garrison are part of the beginnings of our shared heritage.

This book aims to conjure up that sense of connection, a sense of a common spirit of a people and their land. Soak in the ethereal magic of the images – delight in the play of light. These mighty spellbinding skies must have been as vivid to Roman eyes as to our contemporary gaze. They are much older than the Wall that they so dramatically frame. Roger has used his astute photographer's judgement to capture a distinctive radiance and atmosphere, always in the right place at right time, and often before the first lark has sung.

THE ROMAN EXPEDITION to the land of the Britons must have been as daunting as David Livingstone's up the Zambezi into darkest Africa. Apart from trading links with Cornish tin, contemporary Roman knowledge of Britain was unreliable and only gave rise to fear. From the time of Julius Caesar's first visit to the nearest corner of these islands, 90 years were to elapse before the Romans arrived

en masse in AD54 with conquest in mind. Gaul's tentative trading links with south-east England were one thing, but the ambition to subsume the entire islands of Britain into the Empire quite another! Indeed, it was only Agricola's expeditionary fleet another forty years later still that discovered that the size of the challenge was much smaller than they feared.

The Roman Empire was built on obedience and strict adherence to military rule. Its armies were rigidly-ordered fighting machines with absolute allegiance to the Emperor. That discipline kept the Empire on its toes and outwardly mobile, with a confidence that knew no limits when the Romans first arrived. The tribes of southern Britain took their bribes and quickly assimilated. Roman roads swept across the land, carving up each fertile plain, and towns were built and country estates established around handsome villas.

But, to the west and north lived a tougher breed of Celt. These kinsmen lived hard lives. Leaner and keener they survived through close-knit allegiances and were wary of strangers, and a line of resistance quickly became apparent. For some time the diagonal line of the Fosse Way was the effective frontier. Eventually settlement expanded, and with it the road system, and York became a major administrative capital for the north. Yet Agricola's adventures came to an abrupt end after his comprehensive victory over the Caledonians at Mons Graupius in AD80. He was recalled from his governorship of Britannia in AD85, largely out of jealousy of his prowess, and any further thought of conquest kicked into the long grass.

The Roman enthusiasm to subjugate the whole Isles, including Ireland, dimmed and a slow realisation began to dawn that there might be a limit to the Roman Empire. For just three years under Emperor Trajan, Hadrian's predecessor, the Empire had reached its greatest girth. Lying at the furthest north-west extremity of that amazing Empire, Britannia was too remote from the main affairs of state. The drawbacks of the climate aside, Roman chroniclers' unflattering descriptions suggest that they were not attracted in the least to the unruly, uncouth Barbarians of the highlands – although whether this might simply have been a pretext not to complete the task of subjugation one can only speculate.

THE EMPIRE WAS CHARTED by its road system, the number of marching days from fort to fort being the crucial measure. A Roman mile was one thousand strides (double-steps), counted on the lead left foot-fall. This calculation, coupled with the movement of trading and supply ships, must have led to the decision as to where the outer limit of the Empire in Britannia should be drawn for best military effect. The geography came to their aid – the isthmus between the Tyne and Solway Firth providing a convenient neck to throttle,

only a modest 80-mile coast-to-coast march. The geology also gave the boundary-makers the gift of the east-west Great Whin Sill fault, a steep north-facing cliff and natural statement of frontier right in the middle of this convenient constriction. So the Wall's precursor – the Stanegate – which linked the two Roman roads running north at Corbridge and Carlisle, proved a solid military line of control.

So why the Wall? First and foremost, a Roman Emperor had to command respect from his armies. Down the ages, rulers have initiated wars in order to prevent rebellions and deflect their subjects' attention from their other woes. In this case, Emperor Hadrian hit on the brilliant idea, not of warring, but walling! His grand design was to busy three legions in a spot of military engineering to make the Stanegate frontier absolutely people-tight. Historians now believe that he made only one visit to Britain and never saw a single stone of the famous Wall with which he will forever be associated. As the chief of such an enormous empire he had many other battles to fight and his latter years were taken up in the east, where he had another wall built, this time around Jerusalem (renamed Aelia Capitolina) from which he expelled the Jews... how history goes round in circles.

Yet, historical record aside, we can imagine Emperor Hadrian nodding with approbation when his friend and newly-appointed governor of Britannia, Platorius Nepos, first introduced him to the Great Whin Sill. One might construct a picture of Hadrian arriving from Gaul sailing up the Tyne to disembark, perhaps close to the site of Pons Aelius, where later a bridge and wall fort were built in his name and honour. He would then have set forth for Coria (Corbridge), by the Stanegate, to Vindolanda from where a short ride north via Milking Gap would have brought Hotbank Crags under hoof. Platorius Nepos may well have given him an extended ride west along the Stanegate to Carvoran, the glistening Solway confirming the link with the west coast.

Might the magnificence of the Great Whin Sill have triggered in Hadrian's architecturally-creative mind the notion of replicating its form from coast to coast as a frontier wall? His governor will have told him about the characteristics of the local tribes and the need to hamper their activities better than could be achieved by patrolling along the road. He might have suggested a control system built with a no-go military zone to the south, where passage through could only be achieved under escort – a chance to monitor people's movements and exact tolls – with each wall fort a base for cavalry and infantry to quell the first signs of unrest in the bleak hill country to the north.

However the decision was made, over the course of ten years from AD122 the three legions XX Valeria, VI Victrix and II Augusta were intensively engaged in the monumental task, first digging the back line Vallum (the large earthwork and ditch running in harmony with the Wall to the south) and then setting up each fort, milecastle and third-of-a-mile turret. Then, section by section, the Wall itself was built, complete with a wall ditch immediately to the north. It was possibly also rendered and white-washed, although the lack of limestone west of Lanercost is the likely reason that the Wall was originally built of turf (with stone turrets) over most of its Cumbrian course.

The map shows the Roman frontier stripped of its all-important roads and outpost forts and orientated from the perspective of the garrisons' umbilical connection with Gaul and the Mediterranean – the supply ships coming into Arbeia (modern-day South Shields).

LEFT:
Early morning autumn mists fill the depressions in the pre-dawn landscape to the south east of Housesteads

BELOW:
The warm colours of a winter sunrise bursting outwards above the latrines at Housesteads

Although Erboracum (York) was the administrative capital of northern Britannia, the fastest and most direct journeys were always by sea.

Although eventually abandoned by the Romans around AD410 the Wall remained a cultural division. Later it became the first border to an emergent Scottish nation, although the Celtic Strathclyde straddled the frontier deep into modern Cumbria and was still extant in the 12th century. The Dark Ages that followed the fall of the Wall were charactised by a re-invention of petty thiefdoms. By medieval times the area was effectively the lawless realm of family clans who paid allegiance, not to the crown, but their own whim – the infamous Border Reivers.

Much as the Vikings did in their sagas, the Roman times spawned heroic figures whose achievements were passed on from generation to generation in tales of derring-do. One in particular stands out above all others – that of the prototype Arthur, carried through the Dark Ages and into romantic myth to the present day. Lucius Artorius Castus was the commander of Sarmatian cavalry

(hailing from present-day Georgia) who were garrisoned on the Wall at Camboglanna (Castlesteads, near Brampton) and later, after a period of duty at Naples, came together at Bremetenacum (Ribchester in the Ribble Valley in Lancashire). The annals record that in AD183 the Wall was overrun by highland tribesmen who swept south to ransack Eboracum, killing the governor and then heading west. Lucius reinforced his reputation as a brilliant military tactician over a series of battles which pushed the Caledonians back to the highland line and allowed the Romans to reclaim the Wall. The Sarmatians' fighting symbol was their sword Excalibur and on his tomb Lucius is depicted with a dragon's-head helmet. Every charismatic leader thereafter bore the title Artorius, corrupted in the vernacular to Arthur. Possibly the first to be so styled died in a Battle at Ardderyd (Longtown, at the head of the Solway Firth) in AD573, the first recorded date in Scottish history, at which Merlin is reputed to have been enraged. To take the speculation further, perhaps Avalon – the Arthurian Isle of the Blessed – might also be corrupted from the Roman Aballava (Burgh-by-Sands)?

THE ROMAN FRONTIER
FRONT-LINE FORTS

N

SOLWAY FIRTH

■ WALL FORTS
1 ARBEIA
2 SEGEDUNUM
3 PONS AELIUS
4 CONDERCUM
5 VINDOBALA
6 ONNUM
7 CILURNUM
8 BROCOLITIA
9 VERCOVICIUM
10 AESICA
11 MAGNA
12 BANNA
13 CAMBOGLANNA
14 PETRIANA
15 ABALLAVA
16 CONGABATA
17 MAIA

COASTAL DEFENCE FORTS
I   BIBRA
II   ALAUNA
III (BURROW WALLS)
IV   GABROSENTUM
V   GLANNOVENTA

□ STANEGATE FORTS
A CORIA
B VINDOLANDA
C (OLD BRAMPTON)
D LUGUVALIUM

CARLISLE

BRAMPTON

HALTWHISTLE

THE GREAT WHIN SILL

HEXHAM

CORBRIDGE

NEWCASTLE-UPON-TYNE

NORTH SEA

DOWN THE CENTURIES the remnants of the Wall have always remained at some level in the regional, if not national consciousness. It has variously been described as the Pict's Wall, the Wall of Severus or just the Roman Wall. Medieval Mediterranean-based portulan charts showed the Solway-Tyne line marked either as a continuous channel or as castle-crowned mountains, perhaps showing a distorted memory of the Wall.

Being able to see this epic frontier in the contemporary landscape may seem a casual matter. After all, English Heritage, the National Trust, the Vindolanda Trust and others have established a fine exhibition in situ, despite the scarcity of original tooled stone at their disposal. But 1600 years have now elapsed since Roman jurisdiction fell away and it is minor miracle that anything has survived to be displayed at all. Anyone who really gets the Roman frontier bug will sooner or later discover, and then extol, the energy and far-sighted wisdom of John Clayton of Chesters House. His impact on the survival of the Wall, particularly of the most awe-inspiring section along the Great Whin Sill, was almost exclusively due to his personal fascination in the mid-Victorian age. When I created The Roman Ring in 2006 – an all-season walking route to complement the Hadrian's Wall National Trail, take some of the intense pedestrian pressure off the monument itself and open visitors' eyes to the wider heritage of the immediate area – I identified Clayton as the first modern-age hero of Wall conservation, and so he is.

Much work has naturally followed since and all the agents for its survival must be praised and congratulated. In 1987 UNESCO formally designated the whole length of the site of Hadrian's Wall from South Shields to the Solway Firth and down the Cumbrian coast to Ravenglass as a World Heritage Site. More recently the concept has been extended to recognise that the British Wall should not be seen in isolation. The German Limes (550km of

Low snowdrifts converge with the Wall before it plunges to the right to reveal Peel, Highshield and Hotbank Crags. The snow reflects the orange glow of the sunrise.

ancient border from the Rhine in the north-west to the Danube in the south-east) has now been included as another key outer boundary of the Roman Empire. And as this is being written claims for the inclusion of the Antonine Wall (63km from the Firth of Clyde to the Firth of Forth in Scotland) are also being considered. The whole project is now known as Frontiers of the Roman Empire and Hadrian's Wall World Heritage Site is only its first expression.

The establishment of a National Trail alongside Hadrian's Wall in 2003 aroused fresh interest in the Wall, giving even greater importance to the World Heritage Site Management Plan, which is regularly reviewed to determine the appropriate development and management for its medium and long-term wellbeing. Fundamental are the activities of Hadrian's Wall Heritage Ltd, set up in 2006 to co-ordinate protection, development and promotion of the Hadrian's Wall World Heritage Site as a model of sustainable tourism and conservation. This includes the management of walking and cycling trails and sustainable transport initiatives. As a cultural destination, the broader area now known as Hadrian's Wall Country is of international importance. While the Great Whin Sill will always seduce the crowds, and as I hope this book will demonstrate, the story of this historic landscape is far wider, deeper and richer than this single, iconic instance of the Roman footprint.

1

WITH THE TIDAL TYNE
SOUTH SHIELDS TO HEDDON-ON-THE-WALL

Wallsend... now shouldn't that be Wall's beginning? In fact, the frontier system's easternmost station was Arbeia, situated at the mouth of the Tyne in present-day South Shields. It was established as a coastal supply-base and first garrisoned by Mesopotamian bargemen, transferring their skills from the Tigris to the Tyne. These were the forerunners of the keelmen with their shallow colliers' barges, remembered in the folk song 'The Keel Row'. The port, an anchorage for Agricola's expeditionary fleet in AD80, grew in importance forty years on as the Wall came into being and kept up a 278-year connection with continental Europe. Today the site, which, at one time, succumbed to the ravages of onrushing brick terraces, has, like Segedunum a little further upriver, been exposed again and now features a fine reconstruction of a wall-fort gate.

Between these two forts the industrialisation of the Tyne is sore apparent, although 'Bede's World' at Jarrow does give visitors a glimpse into the distant rural past and the life of the Anglo-Saxon monastery of St Paul. The Venerable Bede, famed for his scholarship, died in 735 and was buried at Durham Cathedral, his tomb having the inscription 'here lie the venerable bones of Bede'... Subsequently it would seem that some Dark Age historian skipped 'the bones' to give the eminent priest his distinctive tag! Bede's other world was Wearmouth, the present-day Sunderland, where the locals are known to Tynesiders as 'mackems'. The connection with shipbuilding is uncertain but the most likely explanation seems to be along the lines of 'they mackem, we tackem.'

The imposing cranes of Swan Hunter's famous shipyard at Wallsend, which claimed the ground where Hadrian's Wall once reached the banks of the tidal Tyne, are silent and will soon be gone. Sitting in sharp contrast beside them is the vibrant, futuristic and forward-looking exhibition of Segedunum. With precious little of the fort's stonework remaining, the Tyne and Wear Museum Service has created a fabulous visitor experience, and, at the edge of the site, built an imposing replica bath house, with whitewashed walls and rich orange pantile roof. The interior, painted with maritime motifs and fresh colours, even contains a shrine to the Goddess Fortuna.

FACING PAGE:
The brightness of the warm colours, emphasised by the touch of blue, suggests the physical heat of the caldarium, *or hot room, at the bath house within Segedunum Roman Fort*

FROM TUDOR TIMES coal was dug in Tynedale and traded down the coast to London, but only with the invention of steam pumps were the thick seams more fully worked. Wallsend was the scene of one such deep shaft pit and an old print survives showing a flame stack, indicative of the pit's noxious emissions. It is said that Tsar Nicholas I of Russia paid the colliery a visit and, looking down the main shaft, declared "Ah my God, it is the mouth of hell; none but a madman would venture into it!" – the luxury of a privileged birth.

The course of the Wall towards the metropolis of Newcastle can only be surmised today by such names as 'Fosseway' for the ditch-lined Roman military way and 'Walker' which means 'the alder marsh (carr) beside the Roman Wall'.

The city of Newcastle is the throbbing cultural heart of the North-East of England, much of the interest gathered around the Quayside. For all the smart new developments on the north bank, most of the more recent attractions are based in Gateshead: among them Baltic contemporary art gallery, The Sage music centre and the innovative 'blinking eye' Millennium Bridge. Newcastle manages to be sturdy and dignified, as well as famously vibrant and fun. On the north bank, it has two fortresses – St James' Park, for Newcastle United fans, and the Castle Keep. The keep is squarely sited, as is Carlisle Castle, amid a Roman fort, in this instance Pons Aelius – 'the bridge of Hadrian Aelius'.

The prosperity of the 19th century brought huge physical changes to the city. (The last visions of the pre-industrial age and rural outlook survive in the exquisite etchings of Thomas Bewick, who worked in a drawing office at Amen Corner beside the crowned cathedral of St Nicholas.) The Stephenson family's engine works, located beside Central Station, ushered in the age of steam in the 1820s which soon swept away the medieval core of the city. In its stead came the imperious architecture of Richard Grainger and John Dobson exemplified in streetscapes such as Grey Street, rising by the Theatre Royal to the Grey monument.

The city has long fostered the enquiring mind. The Lit and Phil Society library, the largest outside London, is always open and sits at one end of Westgate, right on the lost Wall. Roman heritage enthusiasts can look forward to the Great North Museum, set to open in 2009, which will house the University's Museum of Antiquities' collection of Roman finds from Northumberland and a good slice of natural history from the Hancock collection. The University of Newcastle is also at the forefront of future life thinking

and aims to become a world leader in hybrid embryo stem-cell research for potential cures for such debilitating conditions as Alzheimer's Disease and Parkinson's. Their Centre for Life has a public arena with exhibitions aimed at inspiring people of all ages.

UPSTREAM FROM TYNE BRIDGE the riverside has undergone considerable change over recent decades, all trace of William Armstrong's prodigious hydraulic crane and armament works, for which the swing bridge was built, now lost. Intriguingly Armstrong advocated the use of renewable energy. Declaring that coal 'was used wastefully and extravagantly in all its applications', he predicted in 1863 that England would cease to produce coal within two centuries. As well as advocating the use of hydro-electricity, he supported experimentation with solar power, and believed that the solar energy received by one acre in tropical areas would 'exert the amazing power of 4000 horses acting for nearly nine hours every day'.

The brick terraces of Elswick and Scotswood are also being progressively replaced. High on Benwell Hill, the Roman fort of Condercum has now gone, beneath a reservoir no less, but the temple of Antenociticus and the unusual Vallum-crossing gate sites have survived, now safe within a suburban close. The West Road charging out of the city lies almost full square on the Wall's foundations. Only a few residual portions have been left beside the way in Denton Dene, among which is the only complete Broad Wall-based turret – 7b – standing within the originally intended Broad Wall.

From the Tyne Bridge the river has, over the last century, been dredged from its many channels to a single waterway which runs by Newburn, today a merry scene of recreation. On 28 August 1640 it was far from such. At the Battle of Newburn, during the

ABOVE:
Modern architecture at its best. At night, the Sage Centre resembles a gigantic spacecraft hovering over the Tyne.

RIGHT:
Segedunum Roman Fort sits in the shadow of the now-defunct Swan Hunter shipyard. Both are former giants of their times, whose power and influence have now been consigned to history. But while the familiar Tyneside view of Swan Hunter's massive cranes will soon be a thing of the past, the ancient ruins of the fort will be preserved.

Second Bishops' War, a Scottish Covenanter army led by General Alexander Leslie took on English royalist forces commanded by Edward, Lord Conway. Conway, heavily outnumbered, was defeated, and the Scots went on to occupy the port of Newcastle and obtain a stranglehold on London's coal supply. Charles I had no choice but to agree to a truce, under which the Scottish army in northern England would be paid daily expenses, pending a final treaty of peace. To raise the necessary funds Charles had to call the Long Parliament, thus setting in motion a process that would lead to the outbreak of the English Civil War two years later.

The Tyne's tidal limit comes close to Wylam, from whose colliery a tramway used to carry coal to coke works in Newburn which stood where the popular Keelman pub and Big Lamp Brewery stand today. The tramway boasted the very first twin-drive traction locomotive – Puffing Billy – built in 1812 by William Hedley, running on a track gauge of 4ft 8½in, exactly the width of a Roman chariot's wheelbase.

ABOVE:
The Newcastle/Gateshead Quayside becomes a world of reflections at night. The River Tyne draws long bars of coloured light down from the illuminated walkways, buildings and bridges; the low cloud reflects the glow thrown upwards by the city at dusk.

RIGHT:
Newcastle/Gateshead Quayside is a tribute to great engineering and architecture, old and new. The impressive new structures of the Sage Centre and the Millennium Bridge respectfully echo the curves of their iconic older brother – the Tyne Bridge.

Grey Street, Newcastle, was voted 'best street in the UK' in 2002 by BBC Radio 4 listeners. The splendour and opulence of its majestic buildings, sweeping down towards the River Tyne, is best emphasised at dusk.

This short stretch of consolidated Broad Wall sits beside the busy A69 Newcastle-to-Carlisle road at Denton Dene. How many drivers ever notice this inconspicuous reminder of the ancient frontier as they pull away from the roundabout?

FACING PAGE:
The floodlighting of the Castle Keep in Newcastle against an early evening winter sky heightens the sense of its impregnability and power

After a long absence, the Wall re-emerges at the hilltop village of Heddon-on-the-Wall, curiously surviving its otherwise wholesale incorporation within the 18th-century Military Road. Almost all trace of the stone structure from here to Sewingshields Farm was lost when the Road was built.

Wylam is the birthplace of the railway, one of the most widespread and most peaceful revolutions the world has ever seen. George Stephenson, who developed the famous locomotive The Rocket, was born in this cottage, standing beside the old Wylam Colliery waggon-way – now a cycle track – a modest beginning for such a giant among men.

The low sun obliquely striking the side of Prudhoe Castle early on a summer morning again evokes a sense of the power and presence of these ancient structures

2

ALONG THE BROAD WALL
HEDDON-ON-THE-WALL TO HEAVENFIELD

The westward adventure brings us to long country horizons, with fields of golden corn replacing the red brick terraces. A lattice of hedgerows and rural walls now chequer the landscape. Unshackled from suburbia, the remnants of Hadrian's Wall break free too and make their most confident appearance yet at Heddon – a tantalising hint of great things to come – before another two dozen miles largely barren of the characteristic tooled stone.

Heddon certainly had its moment in history. The name Heddon-on-the-Wall meant 'heather-clad hill beside the Roman Wall' and sited right on top of that hill is the old church of St Andrew. Reputedly it was here, in the year AD630, that St Cuthbert officiated at the wedding of Oswald, King of Northumbria, at the time the joint most powerful kingdom in Britain. Four years on and 14 miles further along the old Roman frontier Oswald enters history with a bang at the momentous Battle of Heavenfield.

A stroll beside the low remnant Wall in Heddon reveals a shallow bend in its course and, at its western end, the medieval adaptation of a pottery kiln. After the departure of the Romans, the Wall did not immediately fall prey to stone thieves, as the years that followed were characterised by a return to timber building. Only with the advent of the great monasteries, defended halls and castles did the stones really start to disappear, carrying on through the medieval era. After this came another pause until the advent of stone-built bastles (or defended buildings), and, later still, the humbler cottage, barn and field wall.

The Wall at Heddon conforms to the ten-foot gauge that antiquarians term the 'Broad Wall'. When they first began the legion working on the early course from Pons Aelius towards Cilurnum simply followed orders and advanced unflinchingly. But over time, it was clearly decided that the time taken to bring stone and mortar on site was too long and the structure was judged to be solid and stable enough at a slightly narrower width of eight feet. The point of change survives and we must wait to see it on the descent to the North Tyne. They had to work fast as they were working in hostile country. The Celtic Brigantes, or Barbarians as the Romans called them, were none too pleased at having their tribal territory severed and the natural order of their lives crazily disrupted, with unrecorded petty incidents an inevitable by-product.

Beyond Heddon the course of the Wall is represented by a road, with faint traces of the Wall ditch in the arable field to its right. Although the modern A69 takes a diagonal swipe through its line, there is little doubting that the Roman line persists. This is the

Military Road, not in itself Roman but constructed after Bonnie Prince Charlie's Jacobite Rebellion of 1745, although it never functioned as the speedy route for marching armies east to west that it was intended to be. It was a mixture of tragedy and triumph for the ancient archaeology of the Wall. To make the road, what was left standing was thrown down to form a coarse metalling, with tarmac later enshrining the foundations for posterity. As the modern trail-walker will notice, the roadside bank can be seen, from within the adjacent field, to contain the odd unconsolidated Wall stone. There is a certain romance in spotting such tumbled Wall masonry (or 'rubble rigg') fallen from ordered grace.

The first out-of-town Roman fort is Vindobala at Rudchester Farm. What a perfect situation for a Wall museum complex, welcoming visitors fresh out of Newcastle. The modern road slices through the middle of this cavalry fort and only the fenced enclosure hints at its original outline. After a sharp dip and a rise we arrive at Iron Sign. Here, a whitewashed dwelling has been built, its striking red roof catching the eye from a distance. There is evidence, found at Milking Gap, that the Roman Wall itself was also rendered and whitewashed, to achieve the same impact. Travellers will notice various place-name references to 'red houses' in the vicinity of the Wall, hinting to traces of pantile roofing that might plausibly relate to lost Roman structures.

THE NEXT LONG SWOOP of the Wall passes the entrance to Albemarle Barracks, home of the 39th Regiment of the Royal Artillery whose current frontier theatres are Iraq and Afghanistan. Crossing the hilltop hamlet of Harlow Hill again the frontier sweeps downhill, this time running through the flooded headwaters of Whittledene. Here sits a set of glistening reservoir compounds. How the Romans would have approved of them! They were masters of water management themselves, as demonstrated by the aqueducts at Housesteads and Great Chesters and the bath houses, water-header tanks and latrines at all their forts. Cleanliness was not a matter of fussy sophistication; disease was then the greatest killer and cleanliness kept soldiers healthy and fit for the rigours of patrol and combat.

Coarse anglers play their lines into these waters, which are also beloved of birdwatchers. The species list is long and lengthening, and includes the sea duck, the Smew, Whooper Swans passing through from northern Russia and Iceland and vagrant Ospreys from Africa. Even an American Widgeon drake has been spotted.

Above Prudhoe on the Military Road and straddling the Hadrian's Wall Path are the Whittledene Reservoirs. The culvert between two of the reservoirs on a still winter dawn creates an intriguing detail.

After the Robin Hood Inn, the wall rises again. (There is a long tradition of the more isolated inns taking his name and he crops up again two chapters hence at Sycamore Gap, with a further modern twist.) Nearby is a telling farm name – Vallum. Traces of the Vallum do remain here, for all the intensive tilling of the area, although there is also a striking Wall ditch to the right of the road, so big that a footpath needs a purpose-built footbridge to cross it. Halton Shield brings the first really stunning example of the Vallum on Down Hill, skipping left and right. Near the first of those Red Houses is the drive entrance to Halton Castle. Here, the irregular surface of the field on either hand of the open drive protects the remnants of Onnum Roman Fort. One can only speculate as to why it was called 'the place of the rock'.

Halton Castle itself is no mean pile. It is a delightful glorified castellated pele tower clearly built of Wall fort-stone. The curious traveller will wish to venture further south along the winding lanes to find the hidden treasure of Aydon Castle. Sir Walter Scott's Waverley novel *Ivanhoe* was brought to dramatic life here in the 1950s film. The English Heritage notice claims this to be the finest example of a defended medieval manor house in England. Perched on a fierce spur above the Cor Burn, the setting attests to the troubled Tudor times of its owners, the Carnaby family.

THE COR BURN flows swiftly on towards the Tyne, its point of arrival coinciding with the site of the biggest stone bridge of Roman Britain. Search in vain today for the ten-arched structure, which long since succumbed to torrent and flood, although recent dredging has salvaged much of its massive tooled masonry. The road it carried was Dere Street, the main Roman road from Eboracum (York) to the Wall and on north to Trimontium (Melrose) and the Antonine Wall.

Adjacent is Coria, present-day Corbridge, with a multiplicity of fascinating detail and museum exhibits, including its famous Lion of Corbridge sculpture. Like so many Roman artefacts this was casually found and incorporated into a domestic situation as a civic water feature. One tenth of the Roman settlement is revealed in a compound west of the modern town. Running through its heart is the Stanegate, the principal east/west Roman road and effective frontier line at the time that Hadrian made his one and only visit in AD122. To this day the tiny lane leading from the town beside the

Aydon Castle is a fine and largely unaltered fortified 13th-century manor house set on the edge of delightful secluded woodland

river and towards the fort is known as Carel Gate, 'the road to Carlisle'. The present Tyne Bridge was the only stone bridge to survive the massive flood of 1771, when 14 other major bridges were taken out, including the great bridge in Newcastle. As a country town Corbridge has every grace – smart shops, hotels and tearooms – with the air of rural opulence apparent. The parish church, again dedicated to the Scottish St Andrew, has a pele tower incorporated into the churchyard wall, the Vicar's Pele, indicative of the dangerous later medieval age of the Border Reiver, where even the parish priest could only sleep safe within his own defended tower.

From the town, the A68 leads north up to the frontier through Stagshaw Common, at one time the scene of the largest open air livestock market in England, the Stagshaw Fair. The arterial Roman road has served as a conduit for all manner of merchants and drovers down the ages. Today there is nothing more than a roundabout, a pub and a garage showroom but the place is known as the Portgate, confirmation of the ancient economic use of the road in the conveyance of trade. At this point the frontier Wall had a triumphal arch, a gateway flanked by massive guardhouses serving the Roman road. This was somewhat unusual as elsewhere on the Wall major gateways were incorporated into forts. Roman milestones leading west were measured from here.

Turning west once more the ground swells over Whittington Fell with striking evidence of the Wall ditch and Vallum on either side of the present highway. The next little community at St Oswald's Head is complete with a travellers' tearoom. Directly after this, a tall wooden wayside cross indicates an island church, well-removed in the middle of the hilltop pasture. This place is known as Heavenfield. It is certainly in a divine situation, surveying dreamily wide Northumbrian horizons, but it is forever associated with the seminal Battle of Heavenfield – a tussle for supremacy between the Anglo-Saxon Christian Oswald and the pagan Celt Cadwallon – which had its beginning here when a rude cross was raised, the bloody encounter reaching its cruel culmination at Rowley Burn, south of Hexham. The act of raising the cross by King, later Saint, Oswald, was described by the Venerable Bede as the first sign of Christianity in Bernicia, the native name for this district.

The present church of St Oswald-in-Lee, sheltering in a ring of mature maples, has become the spiritual home of Northumberland Girl Guide Association, emphasising the powerful pull that this place continues to exert across the generations.

*The richness of the historic sandstone bridge at Corbridge glows
against the blue of the sky and river early on a snowy winter morning*

The brilliance of a winter dawn at Corbridge, reflected in the River Tyne, brings a magical quality to the scene

ABOVE:
Little is left to look at at Milecastle 24, but the rapid accumulation of rime frost on this dull, windy and bitterly cold winter's afternoon is spectacular and dream-like

FACING PAGE:
The warm colours of a cool mid-autumn sunrise at Coria complement the sandstone of this one-time Roman supply station. You can almost imagine that the Roman builders have only just walked off site for their tea break.

RIGHT:
The ragged sky and the light overnight snow emphasise the isolation of St Oswald-in-Lee Church at Heavenfield

*On the road to the Shire high above Hexham the last vestige
of mist is cleared away by the weak autumnal sun*

3

ENTERING CLAYTON COUNTRY
HEAVENFIELD TO SEWINGSHIELDS

The course of the Wall now pitches down in steady stages into the verdant corridor of the North Tyne, passing Planetrees Farm – the name referring to the sycamores that the Romans introduced to Britain. In 1801 William Hutton passed this way on a solo pedestrian expedition from Birmingham, to and along the Wall. He was horrified to happen upon the farmer, Mr Tulip, pragmatically loading ready chunks of Wall masonry onto his cart for a new barn he was building. Hutton pleaded for its preservation and must have managed to save at least one tiny portion but it is easy to understand why any practical man of that time would have seen no harm in reusing a sad heap of apparently insignificant stone. It is only by happy accident that the junction of the Broad and Narrow Wall here survived – an important record of the Roman rethink of the grand design. Lower down another portion of Wall survives at the edge of Brunton House grounds, this time with a turret intact. Like all the turrets west of here, its Broad Wall wings show that it was built in advance of the Wall, and will have therefore had to be awkwardly sewn into the new, narrow design.

The road meets the North Tyne at the handsome Chollerford Bridge (from 'coele' meaning 'gorge'). Upstream the weir holds a great body of water which fluctuates not merely as a result of natural downpours but also irregular discharges from Kielder Water. The valley has great beauty and any traveller who gives themselves the time to look northward will find pleasure in visiting the little communities of Humshaugh, Simonburn and Barrasford and their surrounding countryside. Barrasford is notable for its active whinstone quarry, which shows the eastern trend of the Great Whin Sill, beyond the Wall, bound for the Northumbrian coast and re-emerging dramatically at Bamburgh Castle and Lindsfarne.

TO THE SOUTH, Chesters naturally demands attention, but before crossing the river it is worth considering the valley back towards Hexham. A confined path leads to the eastern abutment of the great bridge which carried the Wall and Roman chariots over the river to one of the most agreeably sited forts on the entire frontier – Cilurnum. The river must have raged through here on occcasion – two great stone bridges succumbed to its force before the end of the second century. The path runs alongside the old railway line to Bellingham, which used to carry the famous Dipper train – the nickname a reference to the fact that it had had the misfortune to be on the Tay Bridge near Dundee in 1879 when it collapsed in a high wind. The engine was subsequently dredged out and

brought back into commission here – obviously made of tough stuff! The faint trace of the Stanegate's ancient ford can also be seen near here, although a bit distant from the Wall. At the southern edge of the village the Hadrian Hotel inn sign is dignified by a depiction of one Primus Pius, the senior legionary centurion. The river draws down below Warden Hill, crowned with a massive Iron Age hill fort, and comes to meet the South Tyne and double its volume at a stroke. This place must always have been a significant landmark.

Just downstream from here, the river arrives serenely at Tyne Green in Hexham. Just as Cilurnum was a favoured garrison location in its time, nearby Hexham is a favoured location today, a well-connected and well-endowed country town. The old town has an air of civic pride, not least through the activities of the Historic Hexham Trust, and is to all intents and purposes the capital of Tynedale. Well set up from the river it boasts a lovely mix of buildings, new and traditional shops and market facilities. The Market Place is overlooked by the Moot Hall gatehouse, and through the arch in Hall Gate sits the Old Gaol. Constructed in 1330, this was the first purpose-built prison in England, and now, as the Middle March Centre, houses the Border History Museum, vividly depicting that terrible era.

The centrepiece of the town, and its parish church, is Hexham Abbey. When St Wilfred built the original Benedictine monastery in AD675, his biographer Eddius described it as the finest building of its kind this side of the Alps. The crypt beneath housed a holy relic, in this instance a fragment of St Andrew's clothing and pilgrims' offerings help fund the shrine. Coria and the Dere Street Roman bridge were quarried for the majority of the original monastic building, perhaps the first large scale use of the remnant Roman masonry. One particular inscribed stone catches the eye in the ceiling of the crypt, recording a rebuild of the *horrea* (granaries) at Coria. When first inscribed it gave the names of Septimius Severus' two sons Caracalla and Geta. The sons were joint emperors, Caracalla based in Rome and Geta holding a roving commission with the army. Jealously was rife and Caracalla had Geta 'disposed of', whereupon his name was, somewhat ineffectively, erased from the stone. The crypt was lost when the present abbey was built and was only rediscovered by accident during rebuilding work in the 18th century. The present parish church has a multitude of historic detail, artefacts and architectural riches, befitting the dignity of a great holy place.

The setting sun beyond the Mithraic Temple at Carrawburgh early one spring evening

HASTENING BACK TOWARDS THE WALL by Warden Bridge, you pass the little church of St Michael with its authentic 11th-century tower. The churchyard contains an unusual manacled grave, a reminder of the grave-robbing activities of resurrectionists, and also the modest grave of John Clayton of Chesters, the first heritage conservationist of Hadrian's Wall. The by-road leads north to come by Chesters Walled Garden, nurturing the national collection of thyme and marjoram, and meets up again with the Military Road. Across the way and belonging to Chesters House, stands a grand Vanbrugh stable block, appropriate for a place that used to be a cavalry fort. English Heritage's Chesters site, from the riverside bath house suite to the low-walled fort compound within the gracious parkland setting, is unique among the Roman frontier forts and a delightful and fascinating place to visit. Of particular interest is the newly revamped museum which houses John Clayton's many discoveries: sculptures, centurial stones, milestones, inscriptions, stone deities and altars all gathered from the span of the Great Whin Sill to Carvoran, including Vindolanda. There is even a small dog of the kind symbolically thrown into wells at their abandonment; this one Clayton found in Coventina's Well at Brocolitia (Carrawburgh).

John Clayton's father began the great house in the late 18th century in the manner of his age by clearing unsightly rubble from the meadows to create an uninterrupted vista towards the tree-lined river. John's classical education later alerted him to the awful folly and, over the course of the forty years from 1834 when he took over the Chesters estate, he set about the recovery of both the fort and many other sites and lengths of Wall all the way to Cawfields. Every Monday of his working week was dedicated to the task, with William Tailford, his foreman, entrusted with managing the on-going excavation and consolidation works.

AS THE MILITARY ROAD CLIMBS WALWICK BANK it rests squarely on the Wall's foundations, as depicted in an etching of 1862 before the advent of tarmac. As it climbs and enters the Northumberland National Park, the landscape changes rapidly from ploughed fields to pasture and we are into a widening landscape of cattle and sheep. Just beyond Tower Tye sit the rough, unprotected earthen banks of Milecastle 29, while to the south, hidden in Carr Edge Plantation, stands a memorial of another kind, to the site of

Baden Powell's first boy scout field camp. Perhaps he was drawn by the Roman romance of ancient scouting from this historic frontier line, potent imagery for the minds of his young charges.

The two adjacent farms, Green and Black Carts, give a clue to contrasting soils, the former sweet and fertile, the latter sour and unproductive. Another two isolated lengths of Wall are passed before the next summit where the land turns abruptly due west. This place is known as Limestone Corner, a misnomer if ever there was, for the rock is tough volcanic whinstone. There is much to appreciate here, not only in the magnificent panoramic view over North Tynedale beyond Chipchase Castle to the distant Simonside and Cheviot hills, but in the immediate foreground detail. The Vallum here is remarkably complete, driven through the uncompromising rock, but the Wall ditch is unfinished. The Wall ditch was the last part of the jigsaw. Here it seems that either the work team threw down their tools and rebelled, or, more likely, Primus Pilus saw the slow progress, diverted the legionaries to more pressing tasks and this bit just didn't get done. It is an enigmatic spot, untouched over all those centuries, with the stones casually perched on the bank. There is even a split stone still in the ditch, possibly pinpointing the last act of Roman endeavour. Notice the Lewis holes, tapered slots cut into the top of

In the autumn the warm sandstone of Brunton Turret blends perfectly into the landscape from which it came

the stones, the biggest of which weighs around thirteen tonnes. A double swivel steel clasp mechanism fitted into the slot enabling the stone to be winched laboriously up by wooden frame. It must have been a monstrous task.

From here, the rising scarp of Sewingshields catches the eye, marking the onset of the Great Whin Sill. The earthwork features are striking along this entire three-mile section and the fort at Brocolitia – 'the place of badgers' – is worth a visit. It was a later addition, built over the Vallum, and seems at first a featureless pasture mound, but beyond is a reconstruction of the Mithraic temple discovered in 1949, set in the marshy hollow at the head of Meggie's Dene Burn. A peculiarly masculine cult connected with bulls, Mithraism was clearly popular with the soldiers of the Roman garrisons as many such temples have been found. Beyond this one lay Coventina's Well, a native holy spring within which were found a massive hoard of Roman coins. It was evidently a wishing well for votive offerings to the Celtic deity. The original stone shrine, which will once have been brilliantly coloured, is now exhibited at Chesters Museum.

*A dark sky threatens beyond the Wall and the farm at
Planetrees early on a cold late-winter morning after a
fall of snow overnight. Late winter and early spring
snow is magical and all-too ephemeral.*

A calm autumn sunset at Planetrees with a hint of mist deep in North Tynedale

LEFT:
*An abundance of
summer red in a field in
North Tynedale*

On a winter's evening, the grounds of Hexham Abbey resemble Narnia

ABOVE:
The remains of the bridge at Chesters are more commonly photographed from the west bank but the view from the east bank of the River North Tyne tells us more about the structure and location of the bridge and reveals more of the bath house

FACING PAGE:
Midsummer sun breaking the skyline from within the Ditch at Limestone Corner – a curious misnomer as this rock is actually basalt

Autumnal sunrise at Limestone Corner, looking north west across gently undulating North Tynedale

A magnificent sunrise captured in the River South Tyne at Haydon Bridge

Broomlee Lough from the high point of Sewingshields Crags as clouds race across the summer sky

4
A GOOD KNIGHT'S REST
SEWINGSHIELDS TO HOUSESTEADS

The Military Road leaves the line of the Wall for the final time at the crossing of Coesike Burn. A solitary turret leads to the first hint of the swelling whinstone ridge and a small walled plantation of sycamores plots the outline of Milecastle 34. After one more turret the scarp is really beginning to take hold. Approaching the wooded ridge-end sheltering Sewingshields Farm, the growing division between the lonelier, bleaker country to the north – within what is now the Northumberland National Park and Border Forests – and the gentler green, more congenial country to the south leading down into South Tynedale becomes ever more apparent. Certainly until the 10th century, and even later further west, the Roman frontier marked a stark natural division between the emerging Scotland and England. This was a time of new settlement, Irish Vikings colonising the uplands and the Anglo-Saxons, arriving shortly after the Romans left, keeping hold of the more favourable valley land.

Above the farmstead the scarp is fully-fledged and so Milecastle 35, on the scarp edge, had no northern gateway, the strict rules of construction for once pragmatically waived. Unlike most Roman structures which, once relieved of military duty, fell away never again to serve a useful purpose, this milecastle was incorporated into the structure of at least three stone and timber longhouses in the 13th and 14th centuries. These were half domestic accommodation, half accommodation for animals, and they were wild times, with the violent age of Border Reiving fast approaching and the simple husbandry of sheep and cattle a potentially perilous lifestyle, calling for sharp-eyed vigilance. The 'farmer' here later built a bastle which evolved into the present-day tenanted farm. Further west along this section of Wall there are also traces of later shielings, shepherds' summer shelters and enclosures.

At last we come to the brow of Sewingshields Crags, a place of legend and romantic myth. Locals to this day believe that King Arthur and his knights lie slumbering in a cave beneath the edge awaiting the call to arms to protect their Celtic land. The crest of the crags is a place of great elation. Simply standing still is an invigorating challenge in the stiff breeze. Slightly north and forward of the general waving line of the escarpment, from this point you survey with a sense of command and authority what the Romans considered the Barbarian lands, with their great lakes. From here you can see Broomlee Lough (an old Irish word for lake). Long before the wholesale imposition of conifers created the dark horizon of Wark and Spadeadam Forests, collectively known as the Kielder Forest Park, the wild country leading north to The Cheviots was crisscrossed by the tracks of drovers and traders. It also attracted the far more unwelcome rogues, outlaws sometimes known as 'moss troopers'. Cattle rustling reivers exploited every fold in this apparent wasteland to evade pursuit.

To the north of forward scarps, with their Roman quarries, a spinal wall defines the forest edge upon an apparently ancient boundary feature known as the Black Dyke. This leads close by Haughton Green bothy, used by the occasional Pennine wayfarer. In future years it may well shelter walkers on the Moss Troopers' Trail, a new route which runs for 20 miles from Carvoran via Simonburn and on down to Newborough, through the solitary country immediately north of the Great Whin Sill and south of the serried ranks of dense forestry.

THE SCARP NOW SWINGS SOUTH and comes down by King's Wicket, traditionally known as Busy Gap from the regular passage of cattle drovers and outlaws from medieval times onwards. The presence of the erstwhile Busy Gap Rogues caused Tudor annalist William Camden to eschew the Wall during his tour of the whole island of Britain in 1599. In *Britannia* he wrote "Verily I have seen the tract of it over the high pitches and steep descents of hills, wonderfully rising and falling. I could not safely take the full survey of it for fear of the rank robbers thereabouts." Such persona non grata will have found their way by Grindon Lough – today the peaceful haunt of many rare birds – onto the Stanegate, a direct link with the Tyne valley, via Newborough, where today the church of St Peter sits within the bounds of an old Stanegate fort. Above the village lay the famous Settlingstones witherite mine, the sole source of the notorious barium meals once used during x-rays. To the south lies Haydon Bridge, a delightful village built around an old six-arched bridge.

From Busy Gap the ridge becomes a wonderful roller-coaster ride over Kings and Clew Hills and Kennel Crags, but the accompanying wall is nothing more than an orderly field wall for this stretch. The Roman Wall returns to sweep across the Knag Burn valley and come into thrilling union with Housesteads. Downstream

FACING PAGE:
A late summer afternoon looking across King's Wicket to the long incline up to Sewingshields Crags under steel grey clouds

From above Kennel Crags the turbulent sky testifies to the ferocious wind on this bright winter day

in the Knag Burn dell is the site of a Roman bath house and the only archaeologically verified Roman limekiln. From the sheer quantity of lime mortar used in the Wall's construction there must have been an abundance of contemporary structures. You can see their 19th-century equivalent in the pasture south of Rapishaw Gap and, at the Stanegate junction above Chesterholm, the handsomely restored triple-arched Crindledykes limekiln.

The Knag Burn gateway in the Wall is an unusual feature, another modification brought about because the fort's north gate lay above an abrupt bank in the scarp, unsuitable for wagons and the swift passage of the fort's cavalry. Known to the Romans as Vercovicium, Housesteads stands on the most imposing site of the whole Wall. The southern slopes are intensely terraced by strip lynchets first cut in the Roman period and functioning through to the 12th century. These narrow cultivation shelves held moisture for growing oats for the cavalry horses. The south gate was adapted by a branch of the Armstrong clan as a bastle, which gave it the name Housesteads, although there was also an 18th-century farmhouse set about the granaries higher in the fort.

When John Clayton acquired the farmland he removed the farmhouse, as well as the string of farmsteads along the line of the Wall from Chesters to Carvoran, and began a period of excavation. He moved the steading to what is now the National Trust site management offices. The interior of the fort is set on quite a slope, with the buildings rising from the commanding officers' house, by the headquarters building, to culminate at the granaries, with hospital quarters adjacent to the west. The barrack blocks do not remain. Many visitors are fascinated by the latrines in the south-eastern corner – tip top specimens of their genre. Outside the south gate lay a considerable civil settlement. All visitors enjoy simply standing in the middle of the fort and casting their gaze around them. The views are extensive, as the images in this chapter exquisitely reveal.

A spectacle of autumnal evening light from Kennel Crags along the Whinsill Fault to Winshields Crags

Early winter sunsets over Knag Burn Gateway and Housesteads

*Walkers at Knag Burn Gateway as a late autumn sunset
unfolds its spectacular light show over Housesteads*

Sheep file across the wintry landscape underneath Housesteads

To the east of Housesteads the Wall separates from the north wall of the Fort. It then twists and drops to Knag Burn Gateway before disappearing over the next snowy rise.

The remains of a column from the Headquarters Building at Housesteads against the backdrop of a small conifer plantation. The early morning autumn sun is just filtering through the tops of the trees illuminating the mist as the sheep contemplate the rigours of the coming day.

Images of a remnant of the Headquarters Building at Housesteads, spanning twenty minutes of sunrise on a cool autumn morning. The melting mists add a timeless quality to the scene.

*The North Gate of Housesteads on a bright snowy winter
morning with Sewingshields Crags in the distance*

A frosty Housesteads as the early evening moon rises over the pillars of the Granary

The bright sun of an early autumn morning spectacularly lights the broken cloud over the Commanding Officer's House at Housesteads from below

An explosion of colour blazes over the Headquarters Building at Housesteads on a frost-encrusted January morning

Hoar frost on a January morning under a low sunrise over Housesteads

FACING PAGE:
*Clouds dispersing over the Granary at Housesteads on
another dramatic winter dawn*

*Ragged winter sky at sunrise over the Headquarters
Building at Housesteads*

RIGHT:
A calm day above what was once the South Gate of Housesteads, later adapted to be a medieval bastle farmhouse. Fog fills the depressions of South Tynedale.

BELOW:
On another calm winter morning the wet stones of the South Gate of Housesteads reflect the colour created by a break in the cloud on the horizon

PREVIOUS PAGE:
The warm colours of a winter sunrise above the latrines at Housesteads

RIGHT:
The Plantation at Housesteads Crags during a day of persistent wet snow which slowly created this winter wonderland

5
ON THE CREST OF A WAVE
HOUSESTEADS TO CAWFIELDS

The next stage in the Wall's westward progress ranks as the most enigmatic heritage experience on the entire frontier. Certainly it claims the lion share of attention and rightly so. Not only is there the partially paved National Trail along this stretch but also the pasture turf Roman Military Way offers an alternative route on the southern slope, popularly used for circular walks. It's not possible to get any more intimate with the Wall than you do on leaving the fort to the west and entering Housesteads Plantation. For this one brief moment the footpath strides high along the top of a section of suitably stengthened Clayton Wall and, through the branches, you can look imperiously over the whinstone edge into the depths of Barbarian country.

The Clayton Wall, unlike the modern consolidated lengths variously encountered, was one man's solution to a finite supply of authentic rubble. During the mid-Victorian era, John Clayton employed a work team to reinvent the Wall in situ piecemeal from the immediate remaining rubble rigg. Using the, at that time, rare skills of drystone walling, he deduced a mean sustainable height and stuck to it using all the tooled facing stones lying near, inserted as best as possible and following any clues in the foundations. This produced the occasional slight outward steps with the normal staggered overlap pattern in the regimented courses. The Wall was also decorated periodically with the odd inscribed or graffiti stone, although most of the centurial stones were long lost, having come from an upper course above head height. The middle of the Wall was bulked out with smaller stones and the whole capped with turf producing an aesthetically pleasing and quite durable result, with any occasional collapses over the years smartly restored. But it was never intended as a cat-walk.

The first milecastle after Housesteads is a little treasure. The outline of internal rooms can be seen and its north gate has the first stages of its stone arch in place from which one can gauge the actual height of the complete arch and therefore imagine the scrutinised passage of carts and riders. Again this exit from the Empire was onto a pretty steep north slope! The way forward slinks down steps and rises handsomely onto Cuddy's Crags. The view back from here to Housesteads Crags has featured down the decades as

FACING PAGE:
An iconic view across Castle Nick to Crag Lough and Hotbank Crags as the morning sun conjures up a veil of mist over the low ground and the water

the prime visual statement of the Wall frontier and an iconic image of the Northumberland National Park. From here the onrushing wave of the Great Whin Sill is most apparent, with the snaking line of the Wall and its semi-wild setting of crags and scree, trees and pasture, and the eastern backdrop stretching the eyes into a lost horizon, wreathed in mists and mystery.

The Pennine Way leaves the Wall at Rapishaw Gap. To the north lies an advanced escarpment overlooking the largest sheet of natural water in Northumberland, Greenlee Lough. Called West Hotbanks, this scarp-top simply bristles with historic features from the Bronze Age to and beyond the Roman period. There is even a fort attributed to Platorius Nepos. Perhaps it was garrisoned to fend off Brigante guerrilla raids and protect the legionaries engaged in the Wall's construction? Next along is Hotbank Crag, the name alluding to a former ring of trees. The view west from here over Crag Lough to Highshield Crags and further beyond Steel Rigg to Winshields Crags and, in the distance, the final hills of the Pennine chain, is thrilling.

It is worth leaving the Wall for a while at Milking Gap to venture onto the Barcombe ridge by the Long Stone, a suitable spot to cast an eye over the major Stanegate fort of Vindolanda. The signal station on the summit is a good place to judge the ley-line directness of the Stanegate, striking west from the fort as if along the barrel of a gun, and survey the fort on its sheltered shelf. With the same passion and commitment as John Clayton, the Birley family have created, through the workings of their Vindolanda Trust, a remarkable, continuously unfolding and exciting exposition of the life of the frontier, principally from the period prior to the building of Hadrian's Wall. Year on year excavations keep visitors enthralled, their greatest find to date being a mass of writing tablets, preserved in a bog and sealed by clay. Expertly deciphered at the British Museum, they reveal hitherto unknowable details of daily life, echoes from that dim and distant age giving real humanity to raw stones and faintly discernable earthworks. Might there be similar treasures in some boggy hollow along the frontier? After all, only five per cent of the World Heritage Site has so far been excavated!

Below Vindolanda the River South Tyne weaves a beautiful course. Bardon Mill has its distinctive large-pot Errington Reay pottery works while across the valley is the charming little estate village of Beltingham (pronounced 'beltinge-um'). In the churchyard of St Cuthbert's stand three sacred yews, almost as old as St Cuthbert himself. Close at hand at the mouth of the richly-wooded Allen

Gorge is Ridley Hall, former home of a branch of the Bowes-Lyon family. The National Trust cares for the latticework of paths that thread through Allen Banks and it is an adorable place to roam.

From Milking Gap the Whin Sill scarp climbs to crest the bold cliff of Highshield Crags towering over Crag Lough, whose resident swans lend a surreal grace to a wild place. The coppice of mature pines near the top contains woodrush, an ancient woodland indicator, among its ground flora and the whinstone has its own distinctive flora, delicately influenced by the mineral base, wild chives and wild thyme, maiden hair or spleenwort fern, with mountain parsley-fern clinging to the attendant scree.

After a sharp descent the Wall comes to Sycamore Gap. Archaeologists have long waited for the passing of this ageing tree, impatient to explore the mound of rubble banked up against the Wall in the dip. When a similar mound on the north side was excavated a hoard of coins was revealed. A steep flight of steps lead over Mons Fabricius, named after the eminent German frontier scholar Ernst Fabricius. Passing by the foundations of late medieval shielings, the Wall then reaches the dip of Castle Nick, with its specimen milecastle, number 39, which has the character of a cattle pen – with Blue-Grey and Galloway cattle frequently brushing up to it. The Clayton Wall starts again along the rim of Peel Crags before the ridge falls abruptly to Peel Gap and then climbs to Steel Rigg for another of those iconic views that mesmerises the ceaseless flow of visitors who use the adjacent car park.

Down at the Military Road junction stand the Once Brewed youth hostel and National Park Information Centre, serving this

Wet snow has adhered to the stonework and gate at Milecastle 37 in the soft light of a cloudy winter morning

A sunless but bright and frosty autumn morning captures the delicacy of the autumn tints and hues. A towering cloud grows above Housesteads, Kennel and Sewingshields Crags.

hugely popular southern section of the Park. Also at hand is the Twice Brewed Inn, its name originating from the 18th-century farmer's tendency to brew (and serve) weak ale. Today it never fails to satisfy the traveller's thirst with the sumptuous locally-brewed Inebriatus Ale.

The line of the wall rises from Steel Rigg, marked by a field wall, to the high point of Winshields Crags, the highest point on the Great Whin Sill ridge. Due north and less than a mile distant, beyond Saughy Rigg Farm, flows Caw Burn, draining Greenlee Lough. This is the location of Fond Tom's Pool, the starting point of the amazing seven-mile snaking course of the Great Chesters Roman aqueduct, which deftly courted the contours to supply the otherwise 'dry' fort of Aesica. The big dipper ride of the ridge skips through Bogle Hole and then Caw Gap leads onto a lovely section of consolidated Wall via the step of Thorny Doors, with one portion rising thirteen courses high. After tracing the rim of Cawfields Crags, the old name matching its present-day population of crows, and just short of an old whinstone quarry, the Wall reaches Milecastle 42. Perched at a jaunty angle beside the natural nick of Hole Gap, it is best viewed from the spur climb onto the quarry brow.

Darkness enveloping the sky and Cuddy's Crags as the autumn sun sinks below the horizon

A winter sunrise over Milecastle 37 clearly showing the remains of the dividing walls within

FACING PAGE:
The warmth of a subdued midsummer sunset looking through the north gate of Milecastle 37

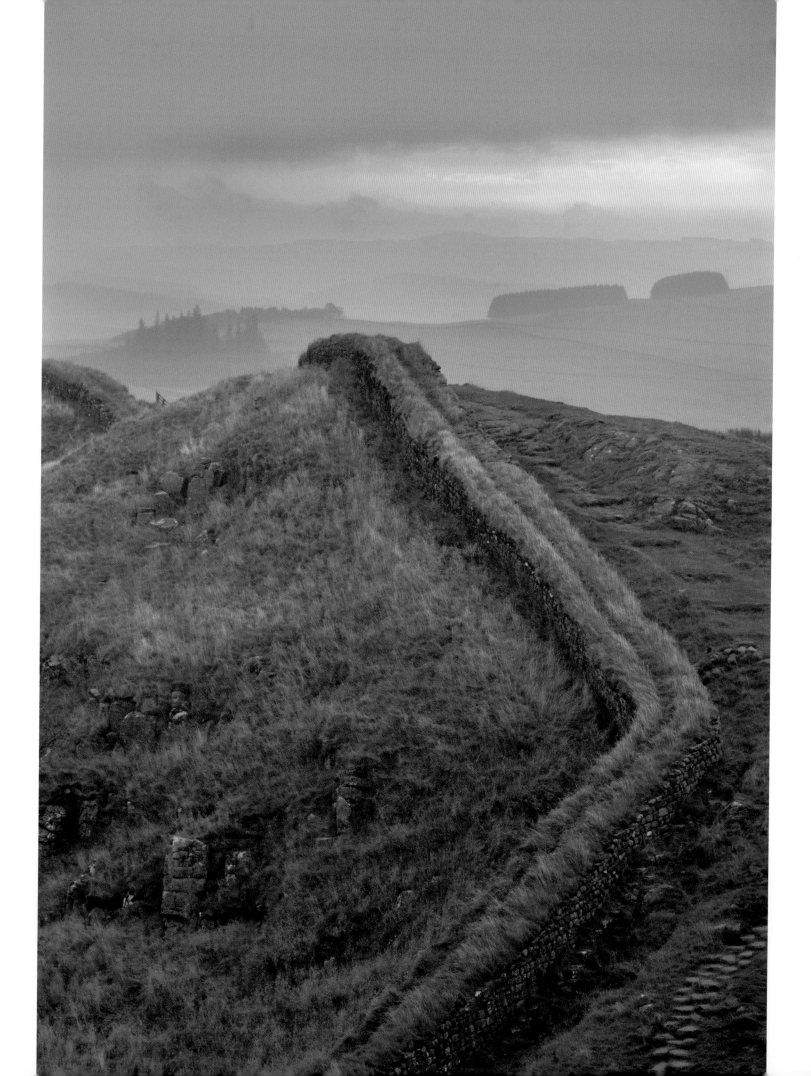

The cloud builds from the north west over Housesteads and Kennel Crags on a cool and blustery early autumn morning

The Wall climbs up to Housesteads Crags. The telephoto lens emphasises the steepness and pulls in the background.

A view to the east of Cuddy's Crags that captures the essence of Hadrian's Wall – the warm colours of the autumn landscape enhanced by the warmth of the sunrise

After a long wait on a cold cloudy morning following heavy overnight snow, a break in the cloud appeared and allowed a weak sun through for a couple of minutes

The Wall snakes its way across Hotbank Crags in the warm light of a low sun late on a cold, blustery and showery autumn evening

FACING PAGE:
The soft light of a muted October sunset high on Hotbank Crags with Crag Lough just visible and Winshields Crags on the horizon

FACING PAGE:
*A wealth of colour as the sun clears away the cloud
on a late autumn morning above the River Allen*

*A wider view from Hotbank Crags across Crag Lough
and Highshield Crags to the North Pennines. The lights
of the Twice Brewed Inn are just visible.*

*Looking towards the monument on Barcombe Ridge and the
North Pennines with a sunset of gentle pastel pinks*

The heavy sky of a cold and gusty December morning with light snow flurries at Sycamore Gap

An intensely cold night at Highshield Crags encased
the rushes with thick frost, but the high white cloud of
an incoming weather system quickly moved across the
sky and the frost was gone

FACING PAGE:
Looking through the south gate of Castle Nick as faint
wisps of cloud radiate out across the sky

*Overlooking Crag Lough from the heights of Highshield
Crags on a cold, blustery morning after a dusting of snow*

FACING PAGE ABOVE:
*A late-summer evening looking past Castle Nick to the
sunset, the chill in the wind signalling the imminent
change of season*

FACING PAGE BELOW:
*The Wall and the new path converge at Castle Nick as they
run westwards on a cold and very windy autumn evening.
The remains of the internal dividing walls are clearly visible.*

To many the view across Castle Nick towards Crag Lough and Hotbank Crags epitomises the Wall. The sun is bisecting the horizon on a midsummer morning.

A cold snowy, winter morning above Castle Nick with Crag Lough and Hotbank Crags beyond. The tracks of a nocturnal traveller run along the Wall.

The dilated early morning spring sun rises through the transient mists over Crag Lough

Crows perch on the stunted trees of Peel Crags with Highshield and Hotbank Crags receding into the mist behind

*Fractured clouds driven by a strong south-westerly
breeze above Vindolanda on an April evening.
The reconstruction of a section of the first fort
can be clearly seen.*

The snow-covered Wall at Steel Rigg leading towards Hotbank Crags on a still winter morning, as the colours of the sunrise spread low across the sky

The Wall and low rippling snowdrifts emphasised by the low sun drop down to Peel Bothy. The Wall and path turn sharply east to the strenuous climb to Peel Crags.

The winter sun highlights moss on the Wall as it curves past Peel Bothy to Peel Crags

FACING PAGE:
Looking down between the Wall and Peel Crags to the ragged early morning sky as the overnight cloud disperses in the wind.

THIS PAGE, FACING PAGE AND PREVIOUS PAGE:
To the east of Steel Rigg is another iconic view of Hadrian's Wall. It includes all the elements of Wall, crags and Lough. I never tire of Steel Rigg; photographs taken from the same viewpoint can vary enormously.

Mist often fills the hollows underneath Peel and Highshield Crags,
but you have to be up early to enjoy its fine-spun beauty

Sleepy sheep awakening early on a misty spring day.
Hotbank Crags and a glimpse of Crag Lough are to the east.

An early morning of pastels, mists and grazing cattle in late autumn at Steel Rigg; South Tynedale and the North Pennines form the backdrop

A crisp autumn morning at Steel Rigg with the last traces of early morning mist under Peel and Highshield Crags

Sheep, not eating yet and seemingly bemused by the overnight snow, under a dramatic sunrise at Steel Rigg

A study in pink at Steel Rigg. While photographing the sunrise I glanced behind to be rewarded by this snowy scene bathed in the light of the early morning sun.

A midsummer dawn from the first warm colours before sunrise until the maturing sun has lost its colour. The succession of crags from Winshields to Sewingshields recedes into the mist.

*The course of the Wall heading east from Winshields Crags melts
into a maelstrom of snow and spindrift on a wild winter day*

*Under an intensely blue winter sky the wind has sculpted
the snowdrift on Winshields Crags into contours*

A late-summer dawn on Winshields Crags shows the Wall
descending rapidly to Steel Rigg, beyond which can be seen
Highshield Crags, Crag Lough and Hotbank Crags

A Dutch family make their way from Winshields Crags to their warm and comfortable overnight accommodation after a day of hard walking

*To the north of Winshields Crags lies Melkridge Common shown here early on
a misty autumn morning. Even today the land north of the central section of
the Wall disappears rapidly into the remoteness of the Border Forest.*

At the end of a midwinter afternoon the sun sinks low into the sky over Bogle Hole, Caw Gap and the beginnings of Cawfields Crags

The early morning sun touches the Wall at Caw Gap, while low cloud glows in the distance over its steep eastward progress to Winshields Crags.

Two rocks stand sentinel over the Wall at Caw Gap

At Cawfields Crags on a bitterly cold February afternoon, heavy cloud and patches
of sunlight are chased across the landscape by a fierce north-westerly wind

ABOVE:
I visited Cawfields Crags for weeks to get a good sunrise with no success, and then, like buses, three came on successive mornings. No picture can ever do a sunrise full credit; this one was awe-inspiring.

FACING PAGE:
Sometimes everything seems to work to your advantage. From an unpromising dawn at Milecastle 42 this dramatic scene unfolded. The strong, low sun highlighting the stones and side of the wall, the heavy sky and the lower layer of wispy cloud illuminated from below conspired to create a landscape photographer's dream. The Spirit of Hadrian's Wall did the work; I was privileged to be there to record it.

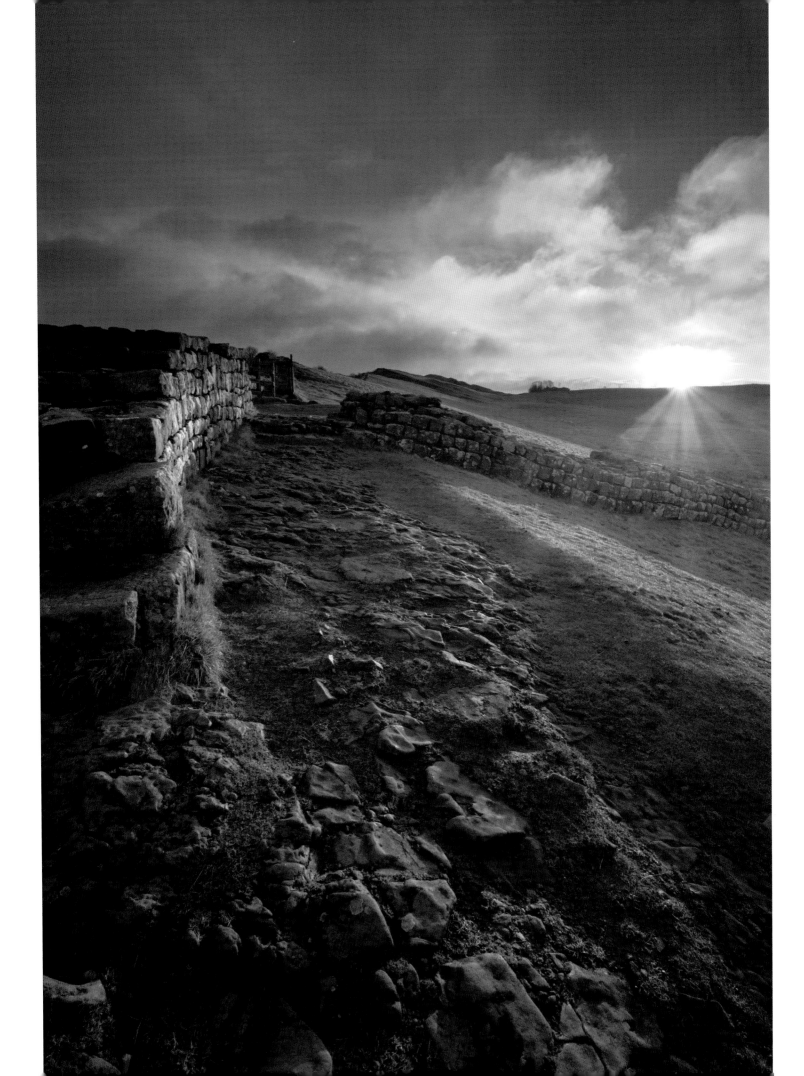

Milecastle 42 under another breathtaking sunrise on an autumn morning

Dawn on a blustery autumn morning at Cawfields Quarry adds another dimension with reflections from the water

A mirror image of a winter sunrise created by the still, deep water of Cawfields Quarry

*Sun breaking through the disintegrating cloud creates a dramatic
sunrise on a late summer morning at Walltown Crags*

6

THE NINE NICKS OF THIRLWALL
CAWFIELDS TO GILSLAND

Haltwhistle is the social epicentre of the South Tyne, far more than a whistle-stop on the Newcastle to Carlisle railway. This former colliery town has roots that chase back to droving times and through the torrid years of Border Reiving, including a visit from Robert the Bruce who put the town to the torch in 1315. A cluster of disguised bastles remain in the vicinity of the Centre of Britain Hotel, so named in recognition of the diametrical equidistance of the town from the coasts of Britain along the cardinal and quadrant lines of the compass. (The information panel in the market square explains the logic.) The town is also famous for the beauty of its surrounding countryside, which walkers can discover by following any one of the imaginative circular routes promoted in a set of leaflets as the Haltwhistle Rings. One such delightful quest is up the Haltwhistle Burn where once a steam-powered aerial ropeway used to run carrying buckets of coal.

Just above Haltwhistle and close to the Wall on the Military Road is the Milecastle Inn. Close by here the coal seams were close to the surface and mined using bell-pits. The intriguing concentration of eight Roman camps above the road and further west on Haltwhistle Common is sure to have used this handy coal and the pits make a fascinating addition to the Roman military mosaic, associated with the period up to the construction of Hadrian's Wall.

The Wall heads west from Cawfields now with the faintest of scarps to Great Chesters Farm. This frontier fort, known to the Romans as Aesica, is entirely agricultural in countenance. There are numerous internal features to see, including the strong room and an informal altar in the south-eastern corner which attracts votive offerings to this day as well as the random rubbings of itchy cattle and horses! The ridge climbs slowly by Cockmount Hill, historically the lekking ground (where cocks compete for the attention of hens) of Blackcock, and reaches the next crest at Mucklebank Crag. The sorry state of the vestige Wall at this point is clearest on the north face – Clayton's presence was sorely missed here.

The succession of gaps between these minor hills have long held the name the Nine Nicks of Thirlwall. Several of the nicks and whole chunks of Wall have disappeared as a result of the zealous extractive consumption of whinstone at Walltown Quarry. In the main the stone was used for town kerbstones, for cities such as Carlisle and Newcastle, and you can still see them in the market square in Haltwhistle.

Within the largest of the 'nicks' issues King Arthur's Well – as at Sewingshields Crag, the fabled 'king' seems to lurk in the longest of

folk memories. The links with the Wall are stronger than many will appreciate, although through the Dark Ages the term Arthur was attributed to many an heroic leader the length and breadth of the land, giving rise to no less honourable claims from Tintagel, Glastonbury and elsewhere. The consolidated Wall weaves handsomely along the crest of Walltown Crags from Turret 45a, originally built as a freestanding tower as a lookout for troops on the Stanegate.

CARVORAN, LIKE VINDOLANDA, had been a Stanegate fort, but unlike Vindolanda was able to step up to Hadrian's Wall duty because of its location. The wooden Stanegate fort has yet to be excavated, although whether it too will reveal writing tablets is doubtful, there being no likelihood of the preserving clay-sealed bog. The Birley family, putting all their showmanship, passion and commitment into the long-term welfare of the Wall story have developed a stirring contemporary show portraying the life of the Roman army through the reels of the 'Eagle's Eye' film. The fort, known to the Romans as Magna, lay at the junction of Stanegate with the Maiden Way, a southbound military road that crossed the Pennines to Brough and passed the unexcavated fort at Whitley Castle, which has received the keen attention of Stewart Ainsworth from 'Time Team'.

Turning its back on the re-adapted Magna, and the dark volcanic magma of the Great Whin Sill, the frontier makes a swift descent to the picturesque ruins of Thirlwall Castle. When Edward I came this way towards the frail end of his life this was a meagre wooden structure. It is unclear when it happened, but at some point in the 14th century Wall-stone was scooped up to build the substantial keep. The name Thirlwall meant 'the hole in the Wall', suggesting a breach that pre-dated the construction of this border bastion and provided access to the Tipalt Burn corridor, a devious back route into Tynedale. General Wade's 18th-century Military Road also tilts down to cross the Tipalt at the village of Greenhead, and today becomes subsumed within the upgraded A69 climbing Greenhead Bank bound for Brampton and Carlisle. Passing the old colliery community of Longbyre, the course of the Wall can be once again detected, as it traverses the Tyne Gap, but only because of the considerable scale of the Wall ditch at this point, there being no trace of stone Wall.

THERE WAS A TIME when people spoke of Gilsland in the same breath as Harrogate or Bath. Towards the end of the 18th century it emerged as a fashionable if modest spa, centred on the Shaws

A soft frosty winter dawn at Bellister Castle near Haltwhistle, with a solitary sheep to share the view

Hotel. Close by the hotel lay the sulphurous well, which had historically attracted all manner of clientele, including Rabbie Burns and Sir Walter Scott. While staying at Wardrew House Scott met and courted Madamoiselle Charlotte Charpentier from Lyons, although one suspects she was unlikely to have been taking the waters. Scott reputedly popped the question at what became known as the Popping Stone in the gorge upstream and the couple married on Christmas Eve 1797 at Carlisle Cathedral.

With the arrival of the railway Gilsland's fortunes rose, as may be judged even to this day by the size of certain pale brick houses, the guesthouses of yesteryear. The railway, the world's first cross-country route, had made it ever more a place of leisurely resort, especially for people seeking some relief, if not cure, from the prevalent ailments of the age. The North-eastern Co-operative Society saw it as an invigorating destination for their many urban members and built a magnificent hotel on the site of the Shaws Hotel in 1859 – still a popular place to stay today.

In 1685 a local vicar found a Roman altar here dedicated to this part of the Roman empire and the health of the Empress. Might the waters once have been taken to offset the worst effects of lead poisoning which so afflicted the Roman ruling classes and sent them mad? Little did they know that it was the shards of lead that they added to sweeten their wine that was the real source of the problem.

Haltwhistle market place in bright, warm summer sunshine

A frosty winter morning looking south east across the
turret high on Walltown Crags into the rising sun

While my camera was set up to record a developing
sunset on Walltown Crags I happened to turn round
and be greeted by this colourful scene, created by the
warm orange light of the setting sun

FOLLOWING PAGE:
*The colours of a glorious early winter sunset on
Walltown Crags are reflected on surface of the Wall*

THE NINE NICKS OF THIRLWALL   151

The Wall dips briefly to the west of the turret at Walltown Crags, revealing the lower-lying, gently undulating countryside to the north

The warm glow of a mid-autumn dawn picks out the sheep grazing on the rough pasture to the south of the Wall. Cawfields Crags and the North Pennines are in the distance.

A raised rocky outcrop and the Wall converge as they run westwards at Walltown Crags. This has always had the potential for an interesting photograph but I visited this location for years before getting the shot I wanted. The prominent rock, the thick frost, the strip of grass, the position of the sun and the broken cloud all came together to produce the impact I had been waiting for.

A train speeds past Poltross Burn Milecastle. How many passengers ever give a moment's thought to this historic site?

Facing page:
I'm always looking for a natural 'design'. Taken from this angle, in this light, these snow drifts and the Wall at Walltown Crags seem to radiate from a single point.

7

STRATH CUMBRIA

GILSLAND TO CARLISLE

The Wall moves on through the post-Roman realm of Strathclyde, over gentle pastures towards the River Eden. Born among the peaty wastes of Spadeadam Forest, the black waters of its tributary, the River Irthing, define Northumberland's boundary here. From Crammel Linn and the serpentine Gilsland Spa gorge it flows through the middle of the village, making Gilsland straddle a regional divide, split in two but paying its dues to Cumbria. The village-name derives from the original Gilbert de Beuth of Bewcastle who owned the estate at the Norman Conquest and to whom the present Earl of Carlisle, Philip Howard of Naworth Castle, can trace his ancestry. Accessed by the Hadrian's Wall Path, tucked up out of sight of the main street, and only fleetingly seen from railway carriages, is Milecastle 48. Its ruins seem to attract romantic attributions. In folk memory it has long been known as Arthur's Stables and even to sober antiquarians it is Poltross Burn Milecastle. More than the usual internal detail survives, but it was only thanks to the geography that the railway engineers missed it.

The track leading to Willowford Farm renews your faith in the physical presence of the Wall as it leads past a turret with Broad Wall wings and then a handsome length of the Wall itself to arrive at the farmyard gate. These days, you can even scrutinise the centurial stone of Gellius Phillippus on the end wall of the barn. A flight of steps leads down from here by the consolidated Wall to the complex remains of the Roman bridge abutment, which is also well worth careful perusal. The river has eaten into the slope of Harrow Scar and left the Roman abutment some distance from the modern stream. Built to last, the modern millennium footbridge, which carries the National Trail here, is a structure of simple grace and beauty.

THE NEXT MILECASTLE SITE is at the top of Harrow Scar. When first constructed Hadrian's Wall was built up to this point in stone and completed the journey to the Solway as a turf and timber rampart. The diminishing sources of lime for mortar this far west and a lack of sturdy stone meant the builders had to revert to the Empire's standard construction model to keep the pace of construction on target. The Romans were scrupulous about schedules and fastidious about following decreed designs, issuing receipts in quadruplicate.

FACING PAGE:

The sun penetrates a thickening steel grey sky at Hare Hill with the snowdrops still shining in the weakening sunlight

Within twenty years of its completion Hadrian's Wall was abandoned in favour of the Antonine Wall but when this was abandoned in turn another twenty years on, the Turf Wall was replaced with a concerted stone Wall, on a slightly different line aiming for the north wall of Birdoswald Roman Fort (Banna). This beelining consolidated Wall is well-endowed with inscribed and centurial stones, including two phallic motifs – charms to avert the evil eye.

It is easy to appreciate the affection many visitors hold for Birdoswald. The setting is altogether far more congenial than the wilder sections on the Whin Sill. Close to the Victorian adapted farmhouse stood the only basilica on the Wall, an indoor drill hall, testimony to the climate, which was later converted into a massive timber-framed hall house. If the Roman history fails to fire your imagination, the view from the southern brink to the great meander of the Irthing will gladden your heart. Heading west, the shallow bank of the Turf Wall next comes above the Comb Crag gorge, a secret scenic treasure, and on the minor ridge-top two turrets are passed, their main appeal being the opportunity to measure for yourself a third of a Roman mile. (The Roman mile was 1,000 paces (double-steps). Count by your left footfall.)

The Pike Hill signal station is worth a closer look. It belonged to the earlier Stanegate frontier system but was incorporated, slightly askew, into the advancing wall and communicated with similar stations on Gillalees Beacon and Barrock Fell. The vista from here stretches down to Blencathra and the Lake District and from the Banks Turret you can cast your eyes towards the northern Pennines of Cold and Talkin Fells above Geltsdale. A renowned RSPB reserve of Hen Harriers and Black Grouse, the Gairs Colliery at its head is reputedly the place where Stephenson's Rocket ended its working life in the 1830s on the Earl of Carlisle's track by Hallbankgate.

AT HARE HILL STANDS A VICTORIAN RE-BUILD, the tallest on the Wall, beating the thirteen courses of Thorny Doors. The landscape becomes altogether gentler now as it passes by Lanercost Abbey. The ruins of this priory church evoke an abiding peace that belies events of the early 14th-century. First, Edward I's year-long stay put a tremendous strain on the Augustinian canons, and then, a dozen years on, the whirlwind raid of Robert the Bruce brought its own mayhem. Wall-stone was clearly 'lifted' by the cartload to build this place and drawn easily down into the valley – a joyous repurposing from the military to the devotional. The bounding wall of the grounds could be mistaken for the handiwork of John Clayton. The

lovely twin-arched Abbey Bridge rests by a fork in the way, left for Naworth Castle and right for Brampton – a pleasing red sandstone town centred on the Moot Hall of 1817 whose market place was set up by the Howards to exploit trade upon the Military Road. The Earl's Victorian patronage of Pre-Raphaelite art and architecture is well represented in the parish church of St Martin and the older church quietly rests a mile distant amid another Stanegate fort.

The passage of Hadrian's Wall by Walton with its aptly named inn, The Centurion, leads on by Castlesteads. The walled garden of this grand country seat, beyond the gaze of casual visitors, sits squarely upon the site of Camboglanna. The fort name meant the meander ('bow') of the Cam Beck. It was a cavalry fort first garrisoned by Sarmatians, a considerable fighting force hailing from Georgia whose vigour in combat became the stuff of Arthurian legend.

By Newtown and Oldwall, on the Longtown road – traditionally the route of the perennially popular Land's End to John o'Groats run – only low ditches hint at the Wall's course. At Bleatarn a long low causeway shows the Wall's foundation passing a bullrush-filled pool, and close by Carlisle Airport. The main road through the village of Crosby-on-Eden follows the ancient Stanegate, evidenced

Bewcastle caught in the calm between heavy snow showers early on a cold late-winter morning

by a short hollow-way, adjacent to the Crosby Lodge country house hotel. Due north of Crosby, a mile or so across the flat pastures of Brunstock Beck stands Scaleby Castle within its ring moat. Built, as one might suspect, of Wall-stone, it played a key role in the first appreciation of the 'picturesque'. The Reverend William Gilpin, headmaster of Cheam School from 1753 to 1777, was the father of the aesthetic notion of landscapes and picturesque ruins as things of beauty. Brought up here he returned later in life and saw the place in a whole new 'framed' artistic light. His 'new eyes' helped promote a new appreciation of the mountains and lakes of his native country – particularly, of course, in the Lake District.

At Walby and Tarraby, two self-evidently Danish settlement names, the Wall draws in, passing by the University of Cumbria's Institute of the Arts, to arrive at Petriana, one of the largest forts on the Wall and one which might well have been the base for the commanding officer of the entire frontier patrol.

The delightful 13th-century St Cuthbert's Church with its red sandstone 7th-century Bewcastle cross, covered in runic inscriptions

*The elegant Willowford Bridge spans the River Irthing.
The course of the river has changed and the remains
of the Roman Bridge are now some distance from the
current course.*

*As disappointment loomed at the prospect of another
sunrise that never was, the sun found a small crack in
the cloud and illuminated both sky and land at the
remains of the Roman Bridge at Willowford Farm*

*On a frosty winter morning the sky mimics the pattern
of the stones on a long straight stretch of The Wall
heading east at Birdoswald Roman Fort*

Looking east past the fortified farm and the fort at Birdoswald into an autumn sunrise

On a dreary autumn morning fissures appeared in the clouds for less than two minutes to mottle the sky with evanescent red

East Banks turret under an eruption of red and blue at sunrise on an autumn day

The early-spring sun rising behind Lanercost Priory

CATTLE GRID

ABOVE:
*The elegant, octagonal
Moot Hall in Brampton*

LEFT:
*The 13th-century Old
Church at Brampton
on an early spring
day punctuated by
intermittent sunny spells
and threatening cloud*

FACING PAGE:
The Gatehouse to Scaleby Castle (a private residence) tells a tale. It is made of spectacular local red sandstone taken from the Wall and displays the heraldic shield of the de Tilliol family.

LEFT:
The raised earthworks are all that remains of the Wall at Bleatarn, Wallhead (local pronunciation 'bli-tarn')

BELOW:
The weir at Cam Beck behind a tracery of lush spring foliage

LEFT:
The illuminated remnants of the outer bailey battlements of Carlisle Castle show the use of stone from the nearby remains of the Wall

FACING PAGE:
The orange cast of the tungsten floodlights exaggerates the red of the local sandstone giving the splendid Carlisle Cathedral an almost cinematic appearance.

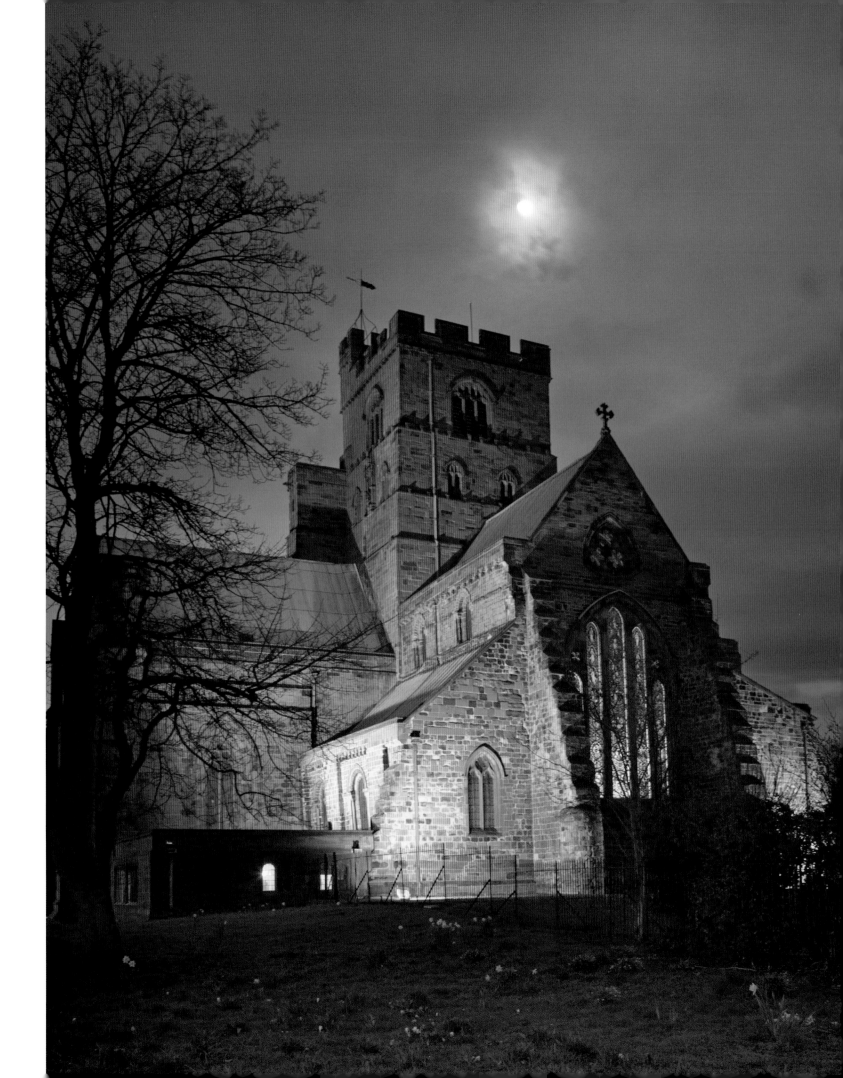

This magnificent statue of a Border Reiver stands defiant and determined on Scotland Road in Carlisle, clear against the insipid sky

8
EDEN TIDE ADVANCES
CARLISLE TO BOWNESS-ON-SOLWAY AND THE CUMBRIAN COAST

'Carlisle – the Great Border City', so proclaim the brown heritage signs in this 2000-year old city, the frontier feeling clearly surviving long after the Roman garrison's departure from Petriana. The modern city grew around the site of the Roman administrative settlement which lay on the raised ground to the south of the Wall's lost Eden bridge. Its name comes from 'caer luel' (city of Lugus) deriving from the Roman name, Luguvalium, which meant 'the wall of [the Celtic god] Lugus'. The keep of the Norman castle sits on Roman foundations and the outer bailey and flanking walls to the once-walled city were, naturally, built from Wall-stone, the eastern wing looking to this day just like a stretch of Wall.

*"Oh, ye tak' the high road, and I'll tak' the low road,
and I'll be in Scotland afore ye"*

The ballad from which this famous couplet comes dates from the end of the Jacobite Rebellion of 1745, when the Duke of Cumberland, henchman of Charles II, rounded up and imprisoned the fleeing Highlanders in the dungeon here. After a public hanging at Harraby, of the few that remained some were transported and a handful pardoned on condition they joined the king's army, which saw the value of their fighting prowess. It will have been the ancestors of these proud fighting men who caused the Romans to draw back from claiming the entire island of Britain... with the help of the midges, of course! Of greater interest to younger visitors perhaps, it was here, in 1568, while under house arrest at Carlisle Castle, that Mary Queen of Scots witnessed the first recorded game of international football. The event was recorded by Sir Francis Knollys in a letter which is now exhibited in the castle keep.

After the castle, the next ports of call for a new visitor, both within five minutes' walk of the castle portcullis, should be the Tullie House Museum – a modern emporium of heritage and culture – and the nearby cathedral and cathedral close. The lack of symmetry in the cruciform plan of the cathedral is striking, the northern cross-wing nave having been truncated after 17th-century Scottish raids.

THE ROMAN BRIDGE over the River Eden also spanned the mouth of the Caldew, annexing the Sheepmount meadow, today split by the mainline railway embankment. Running alongside the old Roman military zone is the sinuous course of the railway, once

that of a canal which linked a basin in Willow Holme with Port Carlisle. At Grinsdale we return to placid countryside once more, its modest church sitting alone above the riverbank, dedicated to St Mungo, the Celtic Scottish missionary and patron saint of Glasgow.

Passing through Kirkandrews and Beaumont (pronounced 'beemont') the Wall kept close order with the Eden which now ebbs and flows with Solway tides. The little church at Beaumont occupies a knoll with a beautiful outlook, as the village name suggests, which was once the site of a Wall turret. Making west across cattle pastures the course of the Wall reaches Burgh-by-Sands (pronounced 'bruff-by-sands'). In fact the sands are quite distant, across more pasture and salt marsh. The Roman fort here, which straddled the village street near the sturdy parish church, was known as Aballava, 'the apple orchard'. A mile outside the village, on the approach to an ancient riding ford to Scotland, stands a railed monument to Edward I, the embittered Hammer of the Scots. In 2007 a bronze statue was erected in the centre of the village to commemorate the 700th anniversary of his death. An effective piece of modern sculpture it is the pair of a similarly majestic depiction of a defiant innominate Border Reiver which now stands in Carlisle, north of the Eden Bridge. Both were financed by local building entrepreneur Fred Story and are the work of John Parkinson of the Upfront Gallery.

THE ROAD TO BOWNESS comes onto Burgh Marsh, which is prone to regular tidal flooding and watched over by the coastguard station at the Dykesfield cattle grid. The Wall cannot possibly have been built either as a turf or stone structure across the marsh. It is likely that the kind of timber palisade on display at Vindolanda, with additional tidal sluices, would have been used. It would have needed regular maintenance and been quickly lost once abandoned. The tiny settlement of Drumburgh was the site of the Wall's smallest fort, Congavata. Drumburgh Castle, however, built by the Dacre family (later Earls of Carlisle) is anything but small – a glorified bastle-cum-pele tower, decorated with Roman altars on the grand stone stairway to the first floor entrance. From the topmost castellated viewing platform unwelcome guests from Scotland could have been clearly seen if they tried to make their way across the Solway mudflats.

At Port Carlisle, facing the mid-Firth confluence of the Esk and Eden, boats used to dock collecting goods and passengers conveyed by canal barge. In the 19th century, many a local family

emigrated to America from here, via Liverpool, among them the mother of US President Woodrow Wilson. The Roman fort at Bowness-on-Solway, now long-gone, was called Maia, 'the large fort', in contrast with the neighbouring diminutive Congavata. Even the fort at Bowness was not the strict end of the stone Wall. Early 17th-century documents refer to traces of foundation as much as a mile further west.

FROM THIS POINT ON, the frontier became a series of coastal defences with milecastles, no less intensively marshalled than their stone, turf and timber counterparts. They ran via Cardurnock then beyond the great re-entrant bay of Moricambe, outflow of the Wampool, and then on from Grune Point via Skinburness and the Victorian resort of Silloth to a fort at Beckfoot. Along this section there is evidence of Roman saltpans and one considerable ceme-tery, which is now being slowly eaten away by the sea. The great fort at Maryport, where the river drains off the Uldale Fells, Back o'Skidda in the northern Lake District, was named Alauna. The Senhouse Museum gives a thorough explanation of this coastal passage and contains a really fine collection of altars and

A pastoral scene of early spring daffodils in the churchyard of St Mary's Church in Beaumont, built on a Wall frontier mound at the precise site of Turret 70A

inscribed stones, including the startling serpent stone and some from the time of the earliest Hadrianic garrison, the First Cohort of Spaniards.

The coastal defences did not end here, although they were less concerted by Moresby. They reached their natural end point at the harbour at Ravenglass. That sheltered haven at the confluence of the rivers Mite, Irt and Esk served as access to a Roman road that traversed the wild fells via Hardknott and Wrynose Passes to Ambleside, linking to a road crossing the High Street range to Penrith, all probably associated with mineral workings, as in the Pennines. Glannoventa, the fort at Ravenglass, has one surviving feature – its bath house – now known as Walls Castle. The walls here are the tallest Roman buildings associated with the Wall frontier – definitely worth a closer look.

This monument to King Edward I commemorates his last act in 1307. In accordance with his dying wish, he was strapped to a horse and rode to face the Scots across the Solway Firth's lowest ford.

The King Edward I monument on Burgh Marsh with Criffel (the big hill) in the background and the sun streaking through heavy evening cloud – a picture of calm and solitude as the Marsh is slowly enveloped in darkness

The stunning statue of King Edward I in Burgh-by-Sands stands resolute and proud, sunlit against the heavy grey cloud

Strong westerly winds working with an unusually high tide
flood the road to Drumburgh and Bowness-on-Solway

FACING PAGE:
The evening sunlight emphasises the texture of the stone at
the charmingly asymmetrical entrance to Drumburgh Castle

*The now-defunct canal from Carlisle enters the Solway Firth at Port Carlisle.
On this magnificent late-winter morning it looked as if the clouds were being
systematically manufactured in Langholm.*

EPILOGUE

Take one last moment to reflect on this remarkable magnus opus pictura. While a photograph may record a blink in the eye of time, what we are witnessing in this unique collection is the result of an ongoing relationship between a shrewd cameraman and his subject. Roger Clegg has come to react intuitively to, and perfectly capture, the many moods of Hadrian's Wall. The environs of this famous stretch of the Roman frontier are the backdrop onto which his lens projects unimaginable, surreal images, each one evoking some element of the spirit of place that we all may crave to experience when we come into contact with this distinctive heritage landscape.

Having pored over these pages, who could doubt that a picture might be worth a thousand words, making this book comparable to Edward Gibbon's 'Decline and Fall of the Roman Empire' in its powers of communication? That dense treatise charted the eras and errors of Rome from Nerva and Trajan through Hadrian and the two Antonines to its ultimate demise. Empires come and go. Whatever remains of them depends on the historical and cultural value that succeeding societies accord them. In the context of the wider Roman frontier, Hadrian's Wall survived by the skin of its teeth. For many centuries its stones were to a large extent untouched, while wood was the preferred building material, and frost was its greatest enemy, but eventually the most obvious stone was removed for other purposes.

The Grand Tour first introduced members of the aristocracy to the buildings of ancient Rome only in the 18th century, so it was not until the mid-19th century that people became interested in protecting the Wall. Then came the first guidebooks, pre-eminent among them being J Collingwood Bruce's 'wallet-book', now in its 14th edition as the *Handbook to the Roman Wall*, whose associated ten-yearly 'Pilgrimage', organised through the Society of Antiquaries of Newcastle-upon-Tyne and the Cumberland and Westmorland Archaeological and Antiquarian Society, still flourishes.

The Roman Wall intrigues on many levels. Strung out across the land it provides a common thread through diverse contemporary landscapes. Where once people approached the frontier with fear and trepidation, today the visitor arrives with a heightened sense of excitement and mystery. Whether you are enthralled by the historic detail or captivated by the romance of the unfolding landscape the truth is that the realm of Hadrian's Wall is a precious and cherished heritage of continued importance and relevance to humanity.

The first time tourist, coming cold to the monument, might be disappointed with the modest array of physical remains set against the greater landscape. This is the challenge of exhibition and interpretation that faces museums and is met by some with controversial replica reconstructions. While the visitor to Housesteads will be spellbound at a magnificent location, the same visitor arriving at Arbeia in South Shields will gain an even more startling impression. Here you can step inside reconstructed buildings, built to scale from gatehouse and barrack blocks according to the grander décor of the commanding officer's residence. At Wallsend you can visit a sumptuously appointed bath house and re-constructed Wall and Vindolanda boasts a replica fort wall, in an attempt to convey the imposing scale of the original monument.

Whether your interest in the Wall is academic or energetic, this book will serve to feed your imagination – a transport of delight to the enduring and timeless Spirit of Hadrian's Wall.

EXPLORING FURTHER

HISTORY BOOKS

Handbook to the Roman Wall (Society of Antiquaries of Newcastle-upon-Tyne 2006) David J Breeze
Hadrian's Wall (Penguin History 2000) David J Breeze, Brian Dobson
Murus ille famosus (That Famous Wall) Depictions and Descriptions of Hadrian's Wall before Camden (CWAAS 2008) William D Shannon
Hadrian's Wall (English Heritage 2004) Stephen Johnson

English Heritage produces further titles to various sites along the Wall frontier, each fascinating dialogues to the greater contemporary understanding. The Vindolanda Trust produce their own exclusive material. There are numerous other treatises and popular guides, but the Wall enthusiast's prime resource must always be the first listed 'Handbook', first published in 1863 by J Collingwood

ABOVE:
The breaking cloud and thinning mist reveal the course of the Wall as it meanders over Housesteads, Kennel and the distant Sewingshields Crags

FACING PAGE:
The ducks obligingly came across the pool at Walltown Quarry and posed for me in front of Walltown Crags

Bruce and still at the leading edge of thought and understanding on the subject of the frontier. The current edition is the meticulous work of Professor David Breeze, recently Chief Inspector of Ancient Monuments for Historic Scotland, following six years of detailed research. Professor Breeze will be leading his third 'Pilgrimage of Hadrian's Wall' in August 2009 on behalf of the combined Society of Antiquaries of Newcastle-upon-Tyne and the Cumberland & Westmorland Antiquarian and Archaeological Society. This will be the 13th decennial 'pilgrimage' studying archaeological developments. The XXIst International Limes (Roman Frontiers) Congress will be held during the following week in Newcastle.

WALKING BOOKS

Hadrian's Wall Path (Cicerone Press 2008) Mark Richards
The Roman Ring (Shepherds Walks 2006) Mark Richards

MUSEUMS

To complement the experience of visiting the Wall itself, there are many museums along or near the Wall that hold a rich treasury of the objects that have been found there and explain the frontier's context to a wide audience. They include the state-of-the-art Great North Museum (opening in 2009) in Newcastle, Arbeia in South Shields, Segedunum in Wallsend, Corbridge Roman Site, Chesters at Chollerford, Housesteads, Vindolanda, the Roman Army Museum at Carvoran, Birdoswald near Gilsland, Tullie House in Carlisle and Senhouse at Maryport.

*Looking west along Cawfields Crags. A break in
persistent cloud cover reveals a sky worthy of
JW Turner – just for an instant.*